The Book of
Pimperne

The Book of
Pimperne

A Millennium Celebration
Compiled by Jean Coull

First published in Great Britain in 2000

Copyright © 2000 Jean Coull
Poems by Barbara Ellis reprinted from *The Green Road*, Aranby Publishing, 1996.

*All rights reserved. No part of this publication may be reproduced,
stored in a retrieval system, or transmitted in any form or by any means
without the prior permission of the copyright holder.*

British Library Cataloguing-in-Publication Data
A CIP record for this title is available from the British Library

ISBN 1 84114 068 6

HALSGROVE
PUBLISHING, MEDIA AND DISTRIBUTION

Halsgrove House
Lower Moor Way
Tiverton, Devon EX16 6SS
Tel: 01884 243242
Fax: 01884 243325
email: sales@halsgrove.com
website: http://www.halsgrove.com

Printed and bound in Great Britain by Bookcraft Ltd., Midsomer Norton.

Dedication
*To the children of Pimperne
and to my grandchildren
James, Beth, Luke
Verity and Tom.*

New Year's Day walk, 1968. Left to right: Bunty Antell, Anne Biles, Doreen Edwards, Mill Waterman, May Malony, Nancy Williams, Jean Coull, Fred Waterman, Bill Coull, Jack Antell.

New Year's Day walk, 1990. The walkers set off on their six mile annual walk across country to The Bugle public house at Tarrant Gunville. Some 13 hardy souls made it to the pub but not all walked back because of the heavy rain. The oldest walker, Mr John O'Farrel, walked both directions.

Foreword

It was a great honour that I should be asked to write the foreword to this remarkable publication. The village of Pimperne is blessed with a great community spirit, as witnessed by the many villagers who supported the compilation of this valuable record. Our forefathers would have difficulty in recognising the Pimperne of the new millennium, but would be grateful that the heart and soul thrives within the community.

This superb book is a testimonial to the past, and a celebration of the future - Jean Coull is to be congratulated for producing such an excellent recording of the way of life, the hopes and the achievements of this delightful north Dorset village.

Della Jones MBE
Chairman, North Dorset District Council.

*Bicycles outside the cottages which are now the Anvil Hotel, c.1930.
Included in the picture are Philip Rose, Ted Dominey, Lloyd Fletcher, Maurice Legge and Jim Thorne.*

THE BOOK OF PIMPERNE

Roy Adam won 1st Prize with 'Black and White Whisky', with his mother Mrs A.D. Adam 'Dionne Quins' at the Coronation Celebrations, 1937.

*Edith Thorne with her daughter at a fête of 1924.
Edith was the eldest daughter of blacksmith Reg Thorne.*

Contents

Dedication — 5
Foreword — 7
Acknowledgements — 11
Introduction — 13

Chapter 1: Early Days — 15

Chapter 2: Roads and Buildings — 21

Chapter 3: The Way Ahead — 31

Chapter 4: The Village School — 39

Chapter 5: Farms and Farming Families — 55

Chapter 6: St Peter's Church — 83

Chapter 7: Pimperne People — 91

Chapter 8: Groups, Shows & Celebrations — 111

Chapter 9: Pimperne Sports Society — 139

Chapter 10: Pimperne and the Military — 145

Subscribers — 157

THE BOOK OF PIMPERNE

Pimperne from the air, February 2000.

ACKNOWLEDGEMENTS

My thanks go to the following who have kindly given information, lent photographs and helped in many ways: Roy Adam, Anne and Bob Allan, Win and Cyril Ball, Myrtle Barnett, Valerie and Peter Boyt, Mike Butler, Margaret Churchill, Barbara Coats, Julie and David Coles, Geoff Coull, Ann Cunniffe, Alan Dennis, Rex Dennis, Irene and John Dowdeswell, Doris and Peter Duncan, Barbara and Rick Ellis, Celia Gilbert, Bernice and Dick Griffin, Phyllis Gulbins, Lady Hanham, Alan Harfield, Sue and Ray Hatchard, Catherine Hewitt, Anne Howland, Betty Jay, Julia Jenner, Connie Johnston, Thelma and Reg Joyce, Colin Kaile, Alice and Stella Langdown, Win Legg, Austin and John Lukins, Gordon Meadowcroft, Sue Miles, Brenda Molony, Jill and Mike Oliver, Jon Parker, Robina Pierrepont, Phyllis Rabbitts, Malcolm Reed, John Ridout, Phyllis Riley, Lynne Saunders, Peter Slocombe, Tim Stankers, Norah Taylor, Jim Thorne, Michael Taylor, Anne and Peter Valder, Millie and Fred Waterman, Micky White, Graham Wicks. I would also like to acknowledge the help given by Dorset County Archives and the Royal Signals Museum.

Cricket dinner at the Crown Hotel, Blandford, c.1960. Left to right, back standing: Doug Cliff, Albert Savage, Michael Wilson, Edward Woodhouse, Keith Barnett, ?, ?, Roy Lucas, ? John Langdown, Micky Ware, Paddy Drennan, Ken Lane, ?, ?, Les Meaden, Tom Barnett; back, seated: Capt. J. Hallett, J. le Pine Hague, Dr Ian Wilson, ?, Dick Griffin, Fred Adam, John Miners, Graham Richards, Oswald Savage, Bob Arnold; front seated: Roy Adam, Tom Hudson, John Shiner, Reg Dennis, Tom Barnes, Ted Barnett.

THE BOOK OF PIMPERNE

Portman Estate Farriers, Reg Thorne (front left) and Frank Jeans (front right) on completing their farrier's course in 1903.

INTRODUCTION

'Life must be learnt backwards and lived forwards'.
(Old Dutch Proverb)

The seeds of this book were sown in the 1970s during long rambles in the surrounding countryside, when much folklore and not a few tall stories were exchanged. Amongst our group was Jack Antell, a gifted story-teller with a wealth of local knowledge, a real feeling for the countryside and generations of local stories. Together we spent the winter of 1977 doing a correspondence course on local history, which involved a lot of research and visits to the Dorset County Archives. The first two chapters of the book are based on this research.

Later Jack went on to study family history, while I did an Open University degree course on Modern European History which led to the oral history recordings in the book, most of which were made in the 1980s. Reading them again now, I realise what a valuable window they provide on a way of life that has all but vanished. Although they are fascinating to record, these oral histories take a great deal of time, and my chief regret now is that many of the village characters of the time went unrecorded.

The book deals mainly with the village of Pimperne, but the parish boundary has changed several times over the years and I have sometimes wandered over the border. Man has made his home here for over 4000 years and families have worshipped in church in Pimperne for over 1000 years. The village grew up along the Winterborne stream and until the 20th century farming was the way of life. Much of the book describes the ever accelerating changes that have taken place in the village over the last century.

Villager Myrtle Churchill as a young girl.

So much was happening in the village in the 1990s that there was little time for writing history! Following a decade of fund-raising and building, we emerged at the end of the century with a new Village Hall, sports field and pavilion and the school also had a much needed hall and gym. The communal effort of all the fund-raising had a tremendously unifying effect on the community, as newcomers joined in with enthusiasm and their fresh outlook and talents were welcomed by a village going flat out to raise the necessary funds.

The offer by Halsgrove to produce a millennium book came at an opportune moment. The chance to record the efforts of the last ten years, put into perspective by the story of the village so far, and lavishly illustrated with memory-provoking photographs was irresistible. Any village history is completely open-ended and every villager will see it from a slightly different angle. One of the things I have found most interesting in compiling this book has been the completely new insights I have gained on familiar aspects of local places and village life.

I have been tremendously encouraged by the enthusiasm of the many people who have helped me with the book – both with reminiscences and photographs. I had not realised before what a deep affection for the place lies in the hearts of so many villagers both past and present. I am particularly indebted to Malcolm Reed and Bob Allan for their contributions on the chapters on the school and church and to Mrs Norah Taylor for the extract from David Taylor's memoirs, to Rick Ellis for his help with photographs and Barbara Ellis, whose poems add another dimension, while no book of Pimperne would be complete without the inclusion of Roy Adam's memories of the village.

THE BOOK OF PIMPERNE

Reconstruction at Butser of Pimperne Iron-Age roundhouse. Here the frame of the building is in place.

The completed roundhouse (courtesy of the Butser Ancient Farm Project).

Chapter 1
Early Days

with contributions from Jack Antell

Pimperne is an old village, which could well have begun its existence with the Saxons c.AD700. The name itself is attributed to the Celtic 'pimp pren' meaning 'five trees'. The parish covers some 3430 acres and lies mostly on chalk at between 170 and 400 feet above sea level. The village stands in a valley running approximately north to south. A number of Anglo-Saxon place names still survive, such as a field close by the village called Links (from the Anglo-Saxon Hlinc, meaning earth ridge). Hyde Farm derives its name for the Saxon measurement of land (hide) sufficient to support one family (usually between 60 and 120 acres). Pimperne gave its name to a hundred in Saxon days, consisting of some 24 698 acres. The Iron-Age settlement on the hill behind the church dates from about 500BC, while the Long Barrow on the northern boundary of the parish near Collingwood Corner is thought to be some 4000 years old and is the most ancient evidence of habitation in the area.

The high ground which surrounds the village is rich in antiquities consisting of the remains of some 17 barrows of the Bronze Age (nearly all of them now levelled by ploughing and only discernible from the air), an Iron-Age settlement, several enclosures - probably of the Iron Age - and a large expanse bearing traces of Celtic fields. We know little of the people who built the Long Barrow on the north-east boundary of the parish, but it is possible that they understood the purpose for which Stonehenge was being erected by their contemporaries some 25 miles to the north.

As far as we know, Pimperne's Long Barrow has never been opened. It is thought to be the largest in the country, being some 108 metres long and 28 metres wide. Some such barrows in the area have been found to contain only a single individual, others up to 50. The bones indicate that the men were up to 5ft 8ins (1.74m) tall and the women 5ft 4ins (1.64m) tall, that many had good teeth, but that arthritis was common. These people settled on the chalk hilltop because the valley at that time was too thickly forested for cultivation.

Part of the Iron-Age settlement on Pimperne Down (near Bushes Crossroads) was excavated between 1960-63. The enclosure covers an area of 11½ acres (4.5 hectares) and is bisected by the Pimperne/Stourpaine road. Inside were found the remains of a circular timber house, 42 feet (13 metres) in diameter, with a baked clay hearth. A bronze finger ring, shale bracelet and a quantity of pottery were also found, together with chalk lamps. (A replica of Pimperne's roundhouse surrounded by an operational Iron-Age farm has been created at Butser Hill, near Petersfield, and is well worth a visit.). Not far from the enclosure, to the north east, lie the Celtic fields which follow a gentle south-facing slope towards, and nearly reaching, the wood named Pimperne Fox Warren, each small square field being between a quarter and half an acre in size.

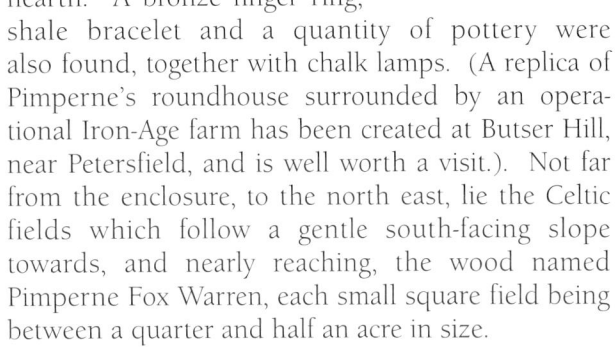

That the land was farmed in Roman times is indicated by the Roman villa at Barton Hill, which lies about a mile and a half north west of the village towards Tarrant Gunville. Roman villas were houses which generally formed the headquarters of large farming estates and implied private land ownership. The villa at Barton Hill was excavated in the 1980s and found to have been built on the site of an earlier Iron-Age settlement. A number of interesting finds are now stored at Wimborne Museum, including coins, pottery and tiles. A great number of oyster shells were also found; it seems that the Romans had a liking for oysters which would have come from Poole Harbour via the nearby Roman road which leads to Hamworthy. In April 1876 the *Western Gazette* reported that a farm lad had unearthed some 50-60 swords, believed to be Roman, while ploughing the field of farmer R. Dominey in Pimperne.

On Salisbury Road just north of Woodyates the county boundary is marked by the earthwork known as Bockerly Dyke, which can be clearly seen stretching across the downs. Late in the 4th century, when Roman power was declining in the face of severe

THE BOOK OF PIMPERNE

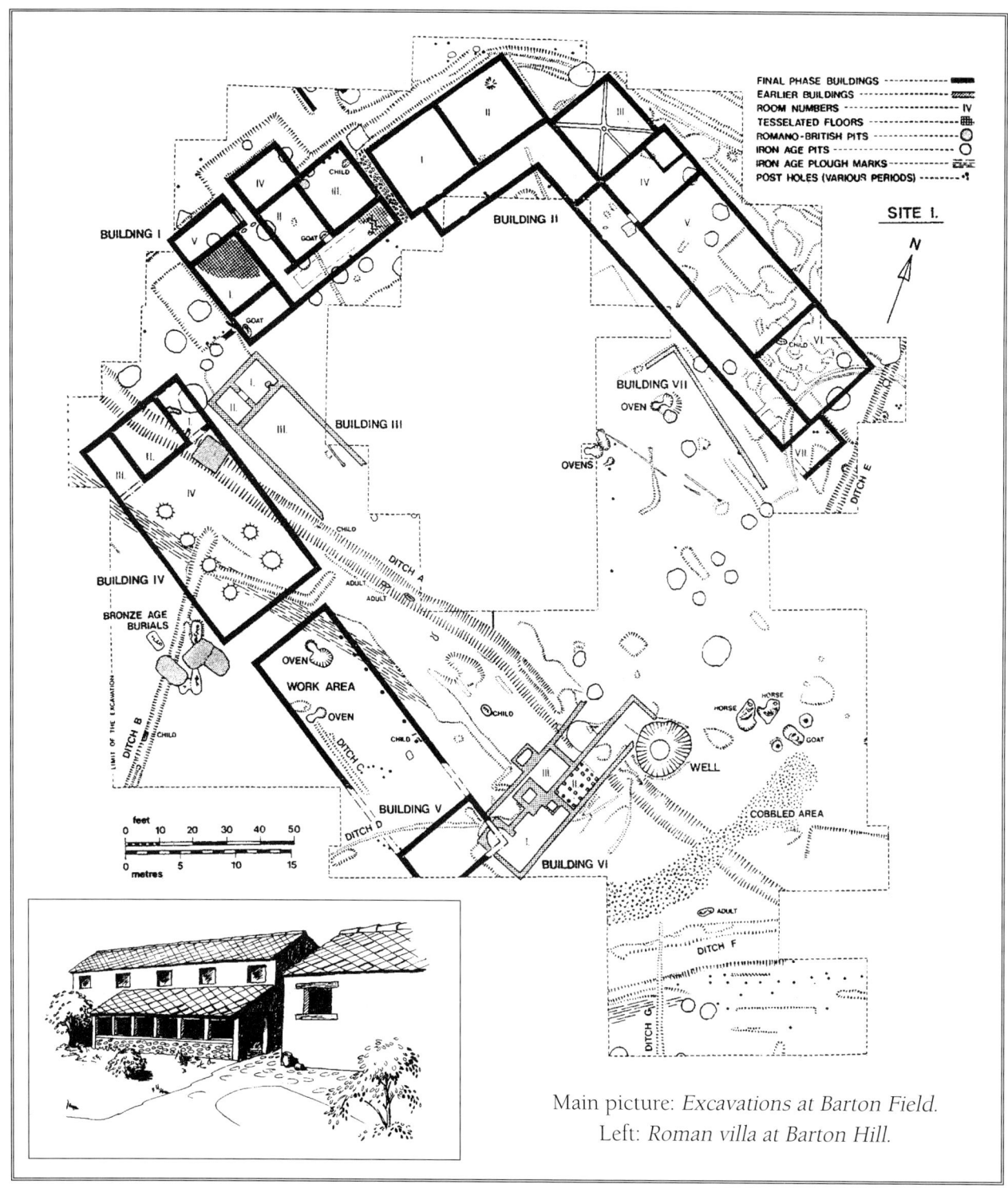

Main picture: *Excavations at Barton Field.*
Left: *Roman villa at Barton Hill.*

Saxon raids all over England, Bockerly Dyke was built to cover the four-mile gap between the forests of Cranborne Chase and the New Forest and to block the great Roman road from Dorchester to Salisbury. This frontier was held until well into the 7th century and behind it the Romano-British people continued for nearly 200 years after the formal end of the Roman period (see C. Taylor, *Making of the English Landscape - Dorset*).

When the Saxons finally arrived the long, patient work of clearing the trees from the valleys began. The old Saxon open fields lay mainly either side of the main road between Pimperne and Blandford, while Newfield Farm (the name is significant) now stands in the slightly later open fields in the north of the parish.

The size of open fields was decided by the number of ploughs in the village and the amount of food required to sustain the community. The Saxons used an eight-ox plough which was so difficult to turn that they made long strips instead of the small square fields used by the Celts. The village today retains its compactness mainly because these open fields were not enclosed until 1814. Two farms in the

EARLY DAYS

village take their names from the Saxon measurements for land, viz. Hyde Farm and Yarde Farm.

It was under the Saxons that our land was skilfully partitioned to meet the agricultural requirements of village communities, thus forming many of the parishes of our countryside as we know them today. The hundreds were formed during Alfred's reign, c.AD890. The name of each hundred generally corresponded to that of the meeting place of the monthly assembly, often a particular barrow or other ancient landmark.

In Norman times the Leet Court was supposed to be attended by the reeve (district magistrate), the local priest and four good men from each village in the hundred, the lord of the manor or his steward. Twice a year there was a special meeting when the sheriff or his deputy attended to check that all male adults were enrolled in tithing groups which took on the responsibility for the behaviour of members.

The parish records of 1740 refer to a field to the west of the church called the Court Close, which had an excavation and a raised bank; there is little doubt that it was here in earlier times the Leet Court was held. It has since been filled in and taken into the churchyard (see Hutchins, *History of Dorset*).

In the Domesday Book (1086) 'Pinpre' is recorded as having '20 Teams, 18 Plough Gangs and 92 males'. In his *Key to Domesday*, the Revd R.W. Eyton observes that Pimperne was deficient in ploughland but had more meadowland than other groups and that the details in Domesday indicate comparative prosperity. It is also pointed out that since the Domesday Book was compiled by William the Conqueror for the purpose of taxing the inhabitants, it is estimated that they only declared about two-thirds to a half of their possessions, so tax evasion is no new thing! The Domesday Book also tells us that Pimperne was one of the manors of the ancient demesne of the Crown from which the king received a fixed rent in kind which was half the 'night's firma' (food and upkeep of the court for a night). In terms of land, Pimperne comprised the equivalent of 5760 acres of pasture, 2400 acres of Domesday ploughland, 720 acres of wood and 8974 acres of grass.

The 94 acres of listed meadowland would have been in the vicinity of the Winterbourne in the valley while the large acreage of pasture would have been the rough grazing on the waste uplands which rise from the village encircling it in every direction except where the valley runs to the south. The ploughland would probably have been any flat area and the lower slopes of the valley. The 720 acres of woodland would have been made up of spinneys, copses and small pieces of woodland dotted here and there throughout the parish. Eastwood, Ashwood and Shawewood have now completely disappeared, lost in time and leaving no trace of their location. Wood must, however, have been a valuable and necessary commodity for fuel, building, and fencing small fields and paddocks.

Spreading outward from the village perimeter the land would have been an unenclosed wide sweep of open country, much of it still covered with scrub and a few isolated trees. This would have been criss-crossed by tracks leading from neighbouring villages, hamlets and outlying farmsteads. The fact that in those days most travelling was done on foot across open and unfenced country meant that people were able to take the most direct route.

As there were 92 males in Pimperne at Domesday and only the adult males were counted in this figure, we can reckon on approximately 40

> ## Pimperne
> A lad in the employ of Mr R. Dominey, farmer, when ploughing in one of his master's fields, suddenly caught his foot against the point of a sword, and on the place being examined, between 50 and 60 swords were found lying in a heap. They were within about the ordinary depth of ploughing, but strange to say, although the field had been ploughed for many years, they had not been discovered. They were all eaten away with rust, and from the formation are believed to have belonged to the Romans.

Map of 1811 showing the fields of the parish.

families, allowing an average of two to a family. (The parish records state that in 1850 there were 124 families living in the parish.)

The houses of this time would have been built of wood or a combination of wood and local flint. There could have been a church - the record of rectors starts in the 13th century, the font dates from the 12th century and the cross outside the church from about 1450. The village at the time of the Domesday survey would probably have comprised one street situated along the Winterborne. Intermingled amongst the houses would have been small paddocks, odd corners of wasteland and gardens, patches of brambles, nettles and weeds which would have lent the whole an unkempt appearance.

This type of habitat would have been favourable for goats and swine, and wildlife would have been plentiful. Birds such as the lark and thrush were caught and eaten in England then as they are on the continent today; rabbits were a serious pest and were dug out of their warrens or caught in nets for food. The untilled wasteland that would today be regarded as an untidy nuisance was a necessary asset to the well-being of the village.

In ancient times the Manor of Pimperne was divided into two parts. The main part was owned by the Earls of Gloucester and Hereford, from whom it passed to the Earls of Ulster, the Duke of Clarence, the Earls of March and then to the Plantagenets, Dukes of York, who brought it to the Crown. In 1540 Henry VIII presented it to his Queen Catherine Howard and in 1543 he gave it to Queen Catherine Parr. During the reign of Elizabeth I it passed to the Ryves family. (The Ryves Almshouses in Blandford, built in 1682, still have one place today reserved for Pimperne parishioners.).

In 1740 the manor was sold to Thomas Baker of Salisbury and in 1767 it was bought by William Portman. This main part of the Manor of Pimperne, which covered most of the village, had remained intact for almost 1000 years. The Portman Estate was split up and sold off in 1924.

The land in the southern part of the parish belonged to the De Quincys. In the 12th century Ralph and Neville de Quincy gave it in pure alms to the Priory of Bremer (Breamore) near Fordingbridge. Part of the land came into the possession of the White Nuns (Cistercians) of Tarrant Crawford. The parish register records that in ancient times at the foot of Priors Lane (Chapel Lane) there was an old wall of immense thickness, doubtless the remains of the old Priory House. At the Dissolution of the Monasteries the Priory of Bremer was divided and in 1543 the land was granted to Sir John Rogers of Bryanstone.

In 1550 Norteford (north ford) was valued at £11. Today it is known as Nutford Farm. France

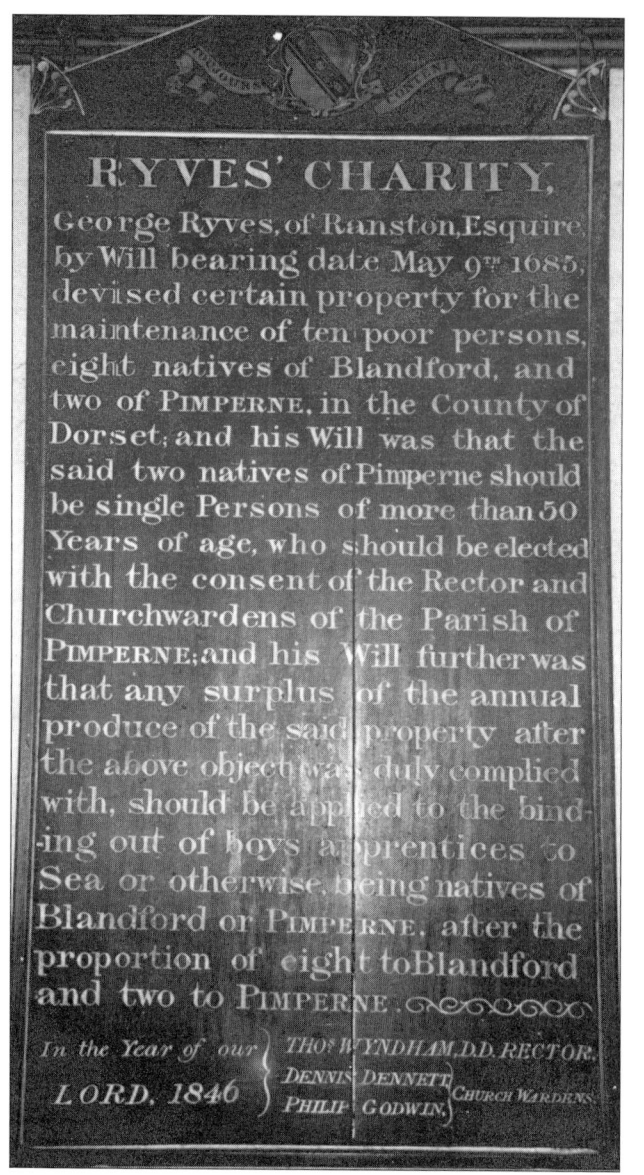

Top: *Church notice concerning The Ryves Almshouses (see sketch opposite bottom).*

Above: *Pimperne Maze.*

EARLY DAYS

Farm was let for 12 shillings a year in 1589 and took its name from a Frenchman who occupied it in Norman times.

Until the end of the 19th century most of the downland which surrounds the village was still unploughed, great flocks of sheep being kept on the pasture of the thin chalk soil. The furze on this land was deliberately encouraged and in some cases planted by the hunting landlords as cover for foxes. The same men were also responsible for the planting of coverts for the same purpose, e.g. Pimperne Fox Warren and Ferns Plantation, but the break-up and sale of the large estates put an end to this practice.

With the advent of war during the 20th century, the downlands came to an end. The need for home-grown food was vital and the turf was turned under - resulting in today's unvaried and monotonous acreage of corn.

Every pond that once existed in the village and surrounding fields has now disappeared. Some were dew-ponds sited by the sides of roads for the use of drovers and shepherds when moving cattle or sheep from the farms to market. One such pond at the side of the turnpike road (now the A354) as the road leaves the village in the Salisbury direction was known as Godwins Pond and was an Enclosure Award in 1814, being designated as a public watering place.

An elaborate and well-constructed maze (*see sketch opposite bottom*) that stood on the corner of the Higher Shaftesbury Lane where the cemetery is now, was destroyed in 1730, although an authentic drawing of the same exists in the vestry of the church. Formed of ridges of earth and stone about half a metre high, it covered nearly an acre of ground.

The church registers date back to 1559. Here it is recorded that in 1850 the parish consisted of 124 families. A parish census in 1850 showed a church attendance of 125 in the morning and 205 in the afternoon, with 95 at each session of the Sunday School. These figures would not take account of those attending the nonconformist chapel in Chapel Lane or any Roman Catholics living in the village.

In 1971 the population of the parish had reached 1160, this being before the boundary change created by the new Blandford bypass when Damory Down and part of Salisbury Road and Philip Road within the bypass were transferred from Pimperne to Blandford. In 1999 there were 839 on the Electoral Roll.

THE LONG BARROW
by Barbara Ellis

Thousands of years ago they came
Herdsmen and farmers, semi nomadic
Leaving so little there is much
To wonder at.
Did small boys watch the half-wild aurochs
As they strayed, grazing the scrubby downs,
While women with digging sticks prepared small plots
For harvest of beans and grass-like grains?
Did they thread the Troy Town maze
With arcane labyrinthine dance –
The dance of Life, penetrating the earth's womb?

Even the maze has vanished long ago
Its convolutions ploughed into the soil,
And only this remains – massive, remote,
The longest barrow of its kind,
Aligned north-south, ditched on either side,
Raised with crude tools by unnumbered men,
An enterprise as staggering as the pyramids,
But more mysterious;
Deep in the chambered barrow lie the bones
Of whom? Kings? Warriors? Priests?
We do not know.

Only that they were here
Long before iron-using Celts,
Settling in the hollow, called the place
The Village of Five Trees;
Before the legions, bringing Pax Romana,
Crossed the downs with military precision;
Centuries before the Anglo-Saxons came
And Christendom replaced the older rites.
These histories are readily constructed
The soil still yields a store of artefacts,
A rich museum underneath our feet.

Yet of those earlier people not a trace
But this –
A turfy sepulchre housing a lost race.

Metalling of Salisbury Road, c.1920 Frederick Adam, landlord, is standing in the doorway of the Farquharson Arms.

Salisbury Road, Old Forge and elm trees, c.1900.

Chapter 2
Roads and Buildings

Today we take good main roads for granted, but the cost of their upkeep has always presented problems. By 1700 little had been added to the road system left by the Romans. In theory every parish was responsible for the roads passing through it and by law each able-bodied man had to give six days labour or money in lieu each year for their upkeep. In practice, however, the work was often skimped and badly directed and road conditions were very bad. It was in an effort to improve matters that the 18th-century Turnpike Trusts were introduced.

The present A354 Salisbury Road came into existence as a turnpike road from the mid-18th century. Before that the road from Blandford had run across the camp to Tarrant Monkton and on to Cranborne, Coombe Bissett and Salisbury. The intended purpose of turnpike roads was to make road users pay for their upkeep. A group of local gentry obtained an Act of Parliament to raise a loan to repair a stretch of road and then put gates across at which point tolls could be collected for its upkeep. The improved road became a mail coach route after 1784. The turnpike roads made the great age of coaching possible on main roads and in 1790 the Weymouth Mail Coach did the journey from London to Weymouth in a record-breaking 18 hours!

However, in the 19th century the coming of the railways bankrupted many of the Turnpike Trusts and put the upkeep of the roads back on the parish rates until 1889 when they became the responsibility of the newly-formed County Councils. The A354 was not surfaced with tarmac until about 1920.

The first Ordnance Survey map for the area, dated 1811, shows that at that time the Higher Shaftesbury Road was an unfenced cattle/sheep drove across the downs. (Blandford, with its lucrative Sheep Market, was a centre for the area.). The present road, which passes the Village Hall to Newfield Farm, in those days led straight on past Keepers Cottage over the hill to Shroton, Shaftesbury and the villages between.

There are perhaps a dozen cob-and-thatch cottages scattered about the village that date from the 17th or 18th centuries, some having had their thatched roofs replaced with tiles. The many disastrous fires of that period led to the building, during the 18th and 19th centuries, of the attractive brick houses banded with flint under tiled or slate roofs. An early example of this style of building is the Old Rectory, which is dated 1712. Reset in the front of the house is part of the 16th-century stone doorway, over which is a shield decorated with the arms of Henry VIII. The earlier house was reputedly a hunting lodge built by Henry VII and part of the Rectory garden is known as Queen Catherine's Walk.

Manor Farmhouse, Chestnut Farm, Little Treddington, Fairfield House, the old school and the Reading Room all date from the mid-18th to mid-19th century. The smaller, but still attractive, flint-and-brick cottages are mostly late-19th century. These were followed by the red-brick school, School House and two farmhouses, now Bowmoor House and Hyde Farm, built in the early 1900s by the Portman Estate.

There is little evidence of building in Pimperne after the First World War and there was an immense shortage of housing following the Second World War. Many homes throughout the land were destroyed by bombing during the war and with servicemen returning to their families there was a determination to provide better housing for the future. St Peter's Close was built immediately after the war, a service being held in the church on 29 December 1946 for the 'Hallowing of St Peter's Close'. The houses were well designed with generous gardens and a spacious green. Unfortunately it was not considered necessary to provide drives or garages as few people had cars at that time. However, times moved faster than anticipated and this attractive close has been somewhat spoilt by the economic pressure on land which resulted in the building of garages and old people's bungalows on the green. Portman Road was another close-type development in the early 1960s followed a few years later by Berkeley Close and Rise.

In the mid 1960s over 100 houses and bungalows were developed on the Stud Farm Estate, followed by the even larger development on Damory Down. However, boundary changes after the building of Blandford Bypass meant that the part of the parish inside the bypass was transferred to Blandford.

Cob-and-thatch cottages (now Anvil Hotel), c.1890.

The Anvil Hotel.

ROADS AND BUILDING

Visible in this picture is Fairfield House (formerly the Laurels) built in 1802 from brick and flint.

Main picture: *Brick-and-flint cottages (Anvil Road) and Bowmoor House, formerly Stud Farmhouse, c.1990.*
Inset: *Horseshoes on stable doors at Stud House, the former racing stable.*

The Old Rectory, c.1910.

Fête at the Old Rectory, 1990.

Pimperne Garage, 1954. The garage was started by Doug Tarr, became Nigel Mansell's garage c.1990 and is now Westover Sports Cars.

The first petrol station in the village was started by Ethel Newbury and is now Pimperne Filling Station. This photograph, 1990.

Anvil Corner, c.1900.

THE GREEN ROAD
by Barbara Ellis

An outspread kestrel rests on air
Then like a missile hurtles out of the sky.
The clean downs sweep away, flint strewn,
Their swelling flanks furred with thin green
Of winter wheat, hedgeless and spare,
Habitat of carrion crow and hares
Galloping in the grip of mating madness.
I walk alone along this old green road,
Rutted and puddled, patched with haphazard flints
This is the natural route into the village.
The packhorse trains must have come this way;
Farmers, back from Sturminster Market, glad to see
The comfortable huddle of roofs in the shallow hollow
Quickening pace downhill to the lane by the stream,
The grey stone church at the heart, its lichened tower
Foursquare and firm, nested in ancient trees
Where rooks roost, villaged above the village.
A few more steps – distance and time converge
Abruptly to the present; the local estate
Still rural in conception, gardens of ample size
With vegetables and chickens, the houses plain
Whitewashed and neat, dwellings of dignity
For the original villagers, rehoused long ago
When we believed Blake's new Jerusalem was here.
Behind them, very new, a multi-coloured stain
Of private houses, neat suburban gardens
Laplock fencing and laburnum trees.
Here newcomers pursue the rural dream
Thrusting their roots into the chalky soil,
The men returning nightly from work elsewhere
The wives meeting for coffee, exchanging recipes.
Between the two communities unease,
Then wariness, and latterly acceptance.
The green road serves us all, for different ends.

ROADS AND BUILDING

*Horse Show in Pimperne, 1930s.
Left to right: Motto Hall, Jack Hansford, Charlie Bishop,
Tom Priddle, Lou Hopkins, Sam Watts.*

Development in the 1970s and '80s included Parr Grove and Fiveways Cottages, Hyde Gardens and Collingwood Close, and these were followed in the 1990s by Old Bakery Close, Yarde Farm and Chestnut Farm. The Village Hall, sports pavilion and a new school hall were all much needed facilities built during the 1990s and which have been proving of great benefit to the village ever since.

With many villages losing their shop, Pimperne is fortunate today in having a thriving, well-stocked Village Store and Post Office. It follows a long tradition. *Kelly's Directory* of 1848 records John Tapper as grocer and baker opposite the Farquharson Arms. By 1907 he had been succeeded by Mrs Mary Jeffery who ran a thriving general store and bakery with several employees. She delivered by horse and trap throughout the neighbouring villages and during the First World War war to Blandford Camp. Tragically, Mrs Jeffery's husband was thrown and killed when the horse bolted.

Max Reeves took over from Mrs Jeffery, and his sons were still baking and delivering bread and groceries in the 1960s. With the new housing developments Franwill Stores in Down Road became the village shop and Post Office, with a hairdressers and soft-furnishing shop next door, followed in turn by the present shop and Post Office in Anvil Road.

The village is well served with public houses. The Anvil started as a tea room in the 1930s and has grown over the past 20 years into an attractive licensed hotel. The Farquharson Arms has been the centre of village activities since the 19th century and has seen many changes. The days when the men finished a hard day's work on the farm and went to the pub for a game of skittles, darts and shove ha'penny have given way to the demands in recent times for the provision of meals and facilities for the whole family, although there is still a formidable darts team!

At the turn of the last century horses were still at the heart of village life, on the farm, in the training stables at Stud House (which achieved fame with a Derby winner in the 1890s) and as a vital means of transport. Joe Dowling, landlord of the Farquharson Arms, was also a horse breaker. Reg Thorne was the blacksmith and Thomas Blandford the wheelwright. The first petrol station in Pimperne (now Pimperne Filling Station) is recorded in *Kelly's Directory*, 1935 edition, as being owned by Ethel Newbury who also had a shop selling sweets, etc. in her front room. Just down the road Eustace Northcote had the Cosy Nook Tea Rooms, with sun umbrellas and an ice-cream kiosk in the garden (now Shepherds Way). After the Second World War Doug Tarr ran a busy garage workshop in Church Road for many years. When he retired this was sold as a sports car garage, famously Nigel Mansell's Ferrari garage. It is now Wessex Sports Cars.

All of the development in the village over the last four decades, together with that of Sunrise Industrial Park, has meant the continuation of a dramatic swing away from an agricultural community which has been gathering momentum since the beginning of the 20th century. In 1900 90 per cent of the working population in the village were engaged in work related to the land; at the end of the century it was less than 5 per cent. By the end of the 1980s it was clear that Pimperne could no longer be called a farming community. A way of life that had developed and adapted over 4000 years had been swept away in the space of one lifetime and the community faced the challenge of finding a new identity.

The Farquharson Arms

Top: *A wagon outside the Farquharson Arms on the Salisbury Road (now the A354), c.1890.*

Above: *The Farquharson Arms, c.1920.*

Above right: *Landlord, Kevin Godfield, 2000.*

Right: *Farquharson Arms, c.1920s, when the landlord was Frederick Adam. The posters advertised programmes at Blandford and Bournemouth cinemas.*

Village Shops

Left: *Farm buildings on Anvil Road, 1970, now the village shop and Post Office.*

Below: *The same scene in 1999.*

Below left: *John Lukins.*

Bottom: *Former village shop and Post Office, c.1990, owned by John Lukins. They all closed in 1998.*

20th-Century Developments

Above: *Yarde Farm development, 1993.*

Right: *Newly built St Peter's Close, 1947.*

Top right: *Old Bakery Close under construction, c.1993.*

Below and right: *View from Bowmoor House to Hyde Farm, c.1980, now Parr Grove and Parr Grove as it is today.*

Bottom right: *Portman Road, 1964.*

Chapter 3
The Way Ahead

In order to cope with the many changes taking place in rural communities in the late-20th century villages were asked to undertake village appraisals – a stock-taking operation which looked at the past, present and future of the village. In June 1988 the Parish Council decided to undertake an appraisal of Pimperne, looking at the history and environment, woodlands, footpaths, etc. which villagers thought important to maintain and enhance, and also assessing future community and social needs. Letters and questionnaires were delivered to all 385 homes in the parish and approximately 500 forms were returned from 272 households – a return of just over 70 per cent.

Children from the school taking part in the village appraisal survey, 1988.

Several areas of need were clearly highlighted. While most people wanted the village to remain as it was, concern was expressed that provision should be made for young people wishing to remain in the village but prevented by the high cost of housing. The most effective way of dealing with this problem was seen as through Housing Association low-cost housing schemes, and in 1993 12 homes were built at Yarde Farm by Magna Housing (*opposite, top left*).

It was felt that Sunrise Business Park, which opened in 1988 was useful in providing light industrial capacity without affecting the residential area of the village. The view was that the site should be restricted to the small starter units originally envisaged and that any attempt to use the site to provide a cheap alternative to larger concerns moving out from the Poole/Bournemouth conurbation should be resisted. It was felt that the site was large enough for the needs of the area and that further development might swamp the village and spoil its rural nature. It was also strongly felt that, in view of the large amount of building that had taken place in the 1980s (for several years the village appeared to be one large building site!), all future growth should be kept to a minimum and that any development to be permitted should, if possible, incorporate an environmental benefit to the village in the form of amenity land, tree planting, footpaths, etc. in order that the rural nature of the parish be maintained. It is still felt to be particularly important that development towards Blandford along the A354 should be resisted, to prevent Pimperne degenerating into an urban suburb of that town.

TRANSPORT By far the greatest demand was for a shoppers' bus that would pick up around the village and go to Blandford; and as a direct result of the survey Damory Coaches started a service to Blandford Market on Thursday mornings. Representations from the Parish Council have more recently provided a Saturday shoppers' bus direct to Poole from the village. A proposed Country Car Scheme received much support and ran for several years but foundered on the increasing form filling required, the final straw being a return to the tax office!

COMMUNITY LIFE There was overwhelming support in the appraisal for a new Village Hall and improved sporting facilities together with the need for a new children's play area. The final question asked: 'Are you happy living in Pimperne?' met with 440 replies: 98 per cent said 'yes' and 9 people said 'no' (of these two said half and half). Under 'comments', 28 people replied that they found Pimperne friendly with a good community spirit. The following was typical:

Pimperne is a very friendly village and help is always available from other villagers for people in need, and getting old is not as painful as it would be elsewhere. The friendly atmosphere of the village in general is something to be maintained and cherished, which makes it a very desirable place to live.

THE BOOK OF PIMPERNE

Parish Council outside the old Village Hall, 1992.

The Village Hall Committee, 1992.
Left to right: Peter Boyt, Peter Slocombe, Fred Waterman, Gordon Meadowcroft, Jack Barnett, Lynne Saunders, Doris Hinton, Jean Coull, Barbara Ellis, Julie Lukins.

THE WAY AHEAD

Pimperne New Village Hall

The old hall, opposite the church, was built in 1832 as the village school and was used as the hall for the village from 1908 when the present school opened. By 1985 the condition of the hall had deteriorated alarmingly due to several years without proper management. After several months of pressure the existing management handed over £250 together with a bill for electric and insurance to the newly-formed Village Hall Committee. The hall was then rewired and repainted, broken lavatories and windows repaired and the kitchen refitted. It became increasingly obvious, however, that a 150-year-old building was inadequate for the developing needs of the village and the 1986 village appraisal showed overwhelming support for a new hall. The cost was originally estimated at £150 000, of which the village aimed to raise £37 500 by fund-raising and the sale of the old hall. In March 1990 an acre of land was donated by the Lukins family as a suitable site for building. However, grants from the County Council had been drastically cut so plans were scaled down.

An exhibition of proposed plans launched the fund-raising campaign in September 1989, a thermometer showed our aim of £10 000, and the first event was an envelope collection around the village which raised £2000. Monthly coffee mornings, the 100-Club draw and bingo evenings became regular events. Plant sales, barbecues, 50-50 sales, cheese and wine parties followed. The big events were an Old Time Fête where over £2000 was raised and 'Gardens Open Weekend' which raised £500. Within a year the target had been achieved. The new hall opened in November 1992, followed by the children's play area a year later. The car park was surfaced in 1995.

Costs of the New Village Hall

Fencing site	£1309
New access across stream	£5250
Building hall	£115 000
Car park	£10 000
Children's play area	£8000
Total	£139 559

The years following the opening of the new Village Hall have seen the flowering of a large number of new activities for the village. Almost 20 different groups meet there regularly for activities for all ages: parent/toddler group, badminton and bowls, yoga, aerobics, the Lunch Club and art and photography groups amongst many others.

While the Village Hall was being planned, work started in 1989 on the new sports field on land donated by the Taylor family and the 1990s became the decade of fund-raising for the village. During these years there were events of every type imaginable – no stone was left unturned! The new sports pavilion and grounds were opened by Mrs Nora Taylor in 1996 and a great deal of credit must go to Barry Hitchin and the team of dedicated supporters who made it possible.

Above: *Old Village Hall, c.1990, built as a village school in 1832.*

Left: *The parent/toddler group enjoy elevenses in the new building. Left to right back: Timothy Baker, Anne Crowley, Jo Sullivan. Included around the tables are: Thomas Crowley, James Fisher Willis, Alysha Truswell, Thomas Sullivan, Darryl Garbutt. The group is run by Sue Randles and Michelle Smith.*

Where There's a Will...

Left: *Village Hall Committee fact-finding visit to Broadmayne Hall, July 1989. Left to right: Lily Barnett, Robina Pierrepont, Betty Ryland, Peter Slocombe, Fred Waterman, Eric Ryland, Jack Barnett, Jean Coull, Doris Hinton.*

Below: *Peter and Doris Duncan at the new hall exhibition.*

Above: *Jack Barnett updating the thermometer, January 1990, the total to that date £3700.*

Right: *Counting the envelope collection, September 1989. Left to right: Barbara Ellis, Jean Coull, Betty Ryland, Peter Slocombe, Peter Boyt, Amy Hayter.*

...There's a Way!

Left: *Model of proposed new hall. Left to right: Fred Waterman, Margaret Churchill, Beryl Edmunds, Jack Barnett, Keith Churchill.*

Top right: *Under construction, 1992. Left to right: F. Waterman, Kevern Snook (builder), Jean Coull, Barbara Ellis.*

Above: *The building is nearly finished, October 1992.*

Above: *Tree planting at the new Village Hall, 1994. Left to right: Jack Barnett, Gordon Meadowcroft, John Ridout.*

Right: *Oh dear, what can the matter be! The carpenter (who was a bit of a joker) caused panic in the village when he announced that a new EEC fire regulation forbade partitions in the ladies.*

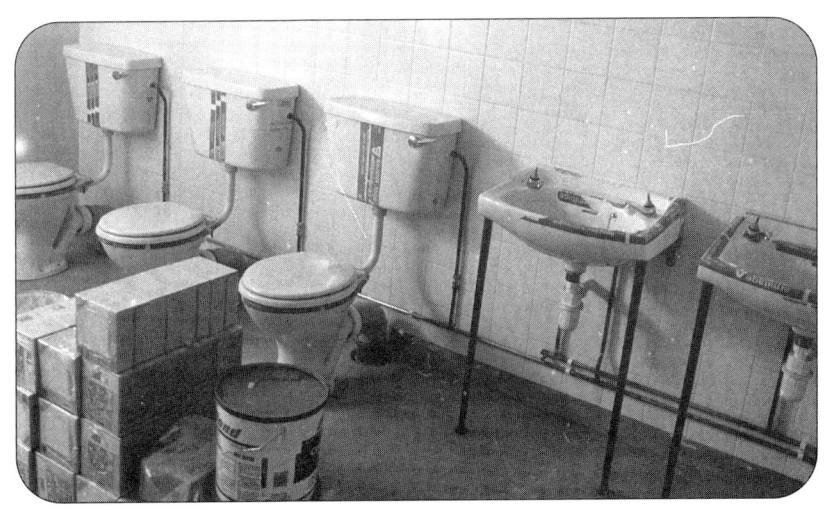

IN 1994 FRED WATERMAN STOOD DOWN AFTER 17 YEARS AS PARISH COUNCIL CHAIRMAN. IT WAS LARGELY DUE TO HIS LEADERSHIP AND FORESIGHT THAT THE NEW VILLAGE HALL AND SPORTS FIELD BECAME A REALITY. HE WAS ABLY SUPPORTED THROUGHOUT BY VICE-CHAIRMAN PETER SLOCOMBE, WHOSE EXPERTISE IN BUILDING WAS INVALUABLE AND WHO TOOK OVER AS CHAIRMAN IN 1994 TO LEAD US WITH A SURE HAND THROUGH THE SUCCEEDING YEARS. THE FOLLOWING ACCOUNT OF PARISH POLITICS OVER THE LAST FEW DECADES COMES FROM FRED WATERMAN IN THE YEAR 2000:

Above: *First Annual Parish Meeting in the new Village Hall, May 1993.*
Right: *Peter Slocombe, Chairman since 1994.*

I came to live in Pimperne early in 1961 and later that year I became a parish councillor under the chairmanship of Albert Lukins, who some years later was succeeded by the local blacksmith, Jack Thorne. They were both fine examples of no-nonsense, practical countrymen and their hands-on approach to local affairs made them very worthy role models for any aspiring councillor. They were indeed men of their time and served Pimperne well. Looking back over nearly 40 years of Parish Council affairs I realise that many of our mundane discussions and decisions have turned out to be important in helping to shape the village we live in today.

In the mid 1960s we were asked to consider an application to house the overspill population from London. This item on the agenda caused much heated comment with many of our parishioners appalled at the prospect of Pimperne becoming another Basingstoke. At a packed public meeting on 19 December 1966 the proposal was given a very decisive thumbs down.

The early 1960s saw the beginning of most of the post-war development within the village; firstly Stud Farm Estate, then Berkeley Rise development, followed by the Berkeley Farm infilling (now Hyde Gardens and Collingwood Close). This last development gave rise to much debate and we gave our approval with much reluctance. Many villagers expressed a wish to retain this area as a landscaped open space - a wonderful idea, but the financial implications shaped our final decision.

Pimperne suddenly became a much smaller village in the mid 1980s when the Boundary Commission re-drew the parish boundaries. The whole of the Damory Down and Larksmead areas were lost to Pimperne - a welcome move that made much sense. People living in those areas never really considered themselves as Pimperne villagers but until this change in boundaries our Council had been asked for comments on planning matters concerning Damory Down. We regularly complained of the proposed density and lack of open spaces. Our observations were not always taken on board but I like to think we made some impact on the final outcome.

Towards the end of the 1980s the Parish Council was pressed into doing something about the sorry state of the old Village Hall. Such was the cost of bringing the building up to an acceptable standard that a decision was made to explore the possibilities of building a new hall. A Village Hall Committee was formed and worked closely with the Parish Council in starting a somewhat formidable project.

Our first task was to establish ownership of the old Village Hall. This proved to be a long drawn-out legal process. The proceeds from the sale of the old hall were needed towards the cost of the new building so we therefore persisted and eventually we were in a position to realise the value of the old building. At the same time a very generous gift of a site for the new building and car park came from the Lukins family. Suddenly our objective was in sight and we were able to open our much-admired hall on 1 November 1992.

Then Michael Taylor approached us with the generous offer of five acres. He said: 'I know the village has always wanted a sports ground and I should like to build at the Mill' - it seemed quite a reasonable planning gain and the rest is history. Within about three or four years we went from a very down-market old hall to a brand new Village Hall, a beautifully surfaced car park, children's play area, a well laid out and re-seeded sports ground and a new sports pavilion.

THE WAY AHEAD

Pimperne Charities

Many people have asked about the origin of the Christmas Cheer distribution: it is a long but interesting story. At the time of the Enclosure Award in 1814 20 acres of land known as Poor Delph situated along the inside of the northern parish boundary, was assigned by the Parliamentary Commission to the overseers of the poor of the parish, the purpose being that they would be bound to preserve and promote the growth of furze on the said area of land so that it could be cut at all times for the benefit of the poor. (This explains the first part of the area's name; 'Delph' meanwhile is an Anglo-Saxon word meaning trench.). At the same time as this allocation was made, the areas of both the parish chalk pit and allotments were confirmed – amounting to one acre and three rods (unit of length equal to $5\frac{1}{2}$ yards).

Poor Delph was used for furze growing for many years, but in 1942 the Dorset War Agriculture Committee took it over for food production at a rent of £5 per annum. It was handed back in 1947 with a demand for £7.10s.0d. p.a. for five years in consideration of the clearing and betterment of the land. Eleven shillings (55 pence) Corn Rent was paid each year to the Church Commissioners but in 1953 they wrote offering to redeem the rental for a total payment of £10.9s.5d. and the trustees agreed.

In 1951 with £62 in the bank the trustees (at that time Mr C. Coats, Mr A. Lukins, Mr Woodhouse, Mr R. Adam and Revd Foxhall Smedley) directed that a sum not exceeding £30 should be divided between old-age pensioners for Christmas. In December 1953 it was agreed to give all OAPs two cwt of coal, the total cost of which outlay would be £16.1s.2d. In 1956 it was agreed to sell the chalk pit to David Taylor for £150, which amount was invested in War Stock bringing an annuity of £7.2s.6d. per annum. Poor Delph was let to Mr Davis for £20 per annum.

The Christmas distribution of coal continued; in 1956 the cost was £20.10s.0d., by 1963 this had risen to £39.6s.6d. At a meeting of the trustees (Mr A. Lukins, Mr Michael de Lancy Wilson, Mr Wray-Cook, Revd J. Foxhall Smedley and Mr R. Adam) in 1963 it was pointed out that many of the recipients had no idea where the coal came from. Revd Foxhall Smedley said that he would write a letter explaining and with Mr Lukins' help would get it stencilled. He would then go around with the coal lorry and deliver one copy of the same to each OAP.

In September 1964 the rent for Poor Delph was increased to £40 per annum and in 1966 the amount of coal being delivered increased to three cwt for a single OAP and five cwt for a couple. In 1967 Mr Davis vacated the land and it was let to Mr Dalton for £120 per annum. By this time the coal distribution was raising increasing problems; the minutes of September 1967 record the Rector, in view of the acute criticism levelled, declining to have anything to do with the ordering of coal and tendering his resignation – this was not accepted and Mr Adam said that he would order the coal himself.

With the development, in 1968, of Stud Farm housing, which was heated by gas, it was agreed that these OAPs should be given a food parcel not exceeding 29 shillings in value (£1.45) from Reeves or Franwill Stores. In 1969 a cash payment of 24 shillings for a single OAP and £2 for a couple was agreed. The rector was to compile the list and organise distribution. In 1970 £1 vouchers for Reeves, Franwill or Rosebank Stores were distributed with a short note explaining who the donors were.

In 1971 it was decided to stop the Christmas distribution and use the money to relieve distress. In 1975 the rent was increased to £200 p.a. and in September 1981 to £400 p.a. Various donations were made and funds built up. Many ideas for spending the money were explored but the trust deed of the Fuel Allotment Charity (*below*), as it was then, precluded the money being used for any purpose other than providing fuel. The steep rise in fuel prices and much larger proportion of pensioners in the village made the task increasingly difficult.

In 1987 the trustees resigned and the Parish Council applied to the Charity Commission for a new trust to be created. Thus the present Pimperne Relief in Need Charity came into being and allowed a wider use of the available funds. The Charity Commission instructed that the income should be used every year and not be allowed to build up as had happened in the past. They agreed that £5000 from the accrued funds should be donated to the new Village Hall to facilitate the setting up of a Lunch Club. The nature of need in the present day differs greatly from the days when the original charity was set up, and isolation and loneliness rather than poverty are the main problems in rural areas. The Lunch Club has proved a successful and popular meeting point.

The charity's income is currently £1000 p.a. and a large part of this is distributed as 'Christmas cheer' in the form of vouchers for the village shop. There are still problems, but it is considerably easier than going around with the coal lorry or walking up to Poor Delph to gather furze!

THE BOOK OF PIMPERNE

Maypole dancing, summer 1992.

Playtime, May 2000. Included in the picture are George Trickey, Miles ?, Chantelle ?, Sophie Pope and Emma Bessant.

Chapter 4
The Village School
by Malcolm Reed with Ann Cunniffe

I arrived in Pimperne in April 1965. The entry in the school's logbook reads: 'I, Douglas Malcolm Reed, commence duties as headmaster.' Thus was marked my first day at St Peter's Voluntary Controlled Church of England Primary School, a school of 80 5-11-year-olds, in three classes, two accommodated in the main building, the third, the infants, in a wooden classroom called a terrapin, a 'temporary' building which is still being used at the time of writing, the year 2000.

There were two other teachers, Mrs Millie Waterman who taught the infants, and Mrs Marjory Fuller, who was responsible for the middle age-group, the 7-9-year-olds. I taught the older age-group. There was no secretary, but this was no problem as the administration was nothing like as onerous as it was later to become.

Mixed age-group enjoying lunch together, 1999. On the front table: Chantelle Evans (plaits), Rachel Goodfield, Amy Collins, Helen Miller, Verity Ockenden, ?, Elizabeth Ebury, Hannah Stroud; on the back table: Christopher Moggridge, Adam Oliver, Christopher Sanderson, Miles Keatley.

The logbook referred to above was also known as a diary, and into it every school was required to enter a bare record of events which constituted the history of the school. Entries were to be made by the headteacher as the occasion arose. The first entry in Pimperne School's logbook was on 21 December 1917, the entry having been made by the then headmaster, Mr W. Fry. Incidentally, each school also had to keep a punishment book in which all cases of corporal punishment were to be recorded, an admission register and attendance registers. Older teachers will recall with horror the weekly, monthly and even yearly class attendance totals which had to be completed and balanced at the appropriate times before going home. A discrepancy of thousands resulting from a single figure error wasn't unknown!

Today most regard regular attendance as of the utmost importance but it was not always so. On one day in 1918 it was recorded in the logbook that the attendance was 'so very bad that lessons could not be in accordance with the timetable'. A list of pupils who attended badly shows that 34 of them out of a total of about 60 put in fewer days at school than half the required total, and it was often the same pupils whose names appeared on similar lists. Poor attendance was frequently marked 'without satisfactory reason', although working on the farm, haymaking and harvest were often quoted. However, on one occasion, five boys were absent 'acting as caddies on the golf links'.

Bad weather, heavy rain and sickness were given as excuses for poor attendances. There were occasions when epidemics decimated the numbers attending - many of which we seldom hear of today, including diphtheria, whooping cough, polio, tuberculosis and impetigo. Today, some of the illnesses mentioned are caused by diet or foreign travel, amoebic dysentery, salmonella, or infective hepatitis; indeed this latter was the cause of all of the teaching and non-teaching staff being immunised in 1970. Regretfully, and it is something we all recall, head lice have once again reappeared with a vengeance.

Possibly the earliest record of a school in Pimperne suggests that there was an Infants' School established in 1827. There were 46 pupils aged from 18 months to 6 years of age. In 1832 Lord Portman provided the building for the National School opposite the church. This was to become the Village Hall and later still a private house. The present school was opened in 1908 and consisted of three classrooms to accommodate about 60 children. The lavatories, or 'offices' as they were more commonly known, were outside - no flushes of course, just sanitary pails which, according to the logbook, were often not 'attended to properly' by the cleaner. Indoor toilets were located in the main building at a later date when these outbuildings became redundant and were used for storage - apart for one, that is, which was retained as a staff toilet!

There is a trust deed dated 16 October 1925, in which it is stated that Lord Portman sold the school and the land on which it stood to the Salisbury Diocesan Board of Finance. The deed goes on to read:

> ... the Board shall hold the premises to be used for... the celebration of divine service... for religious education... for the education of children and adults or children only of the labouring, manufacturing and other poorer classes in the Parish of Pimperne.

Up until the 1970s the accommodation changed very little. Classrooms were heated by coke stoves with an oil heater in the terrapin, but recalling the problems later encountered with central heating, perhaps there was something to be said for these 'antiquated' methods. There was no telephone; any calls, including in an emergency, had to be made from a call box at the other end of the village. A telephone was later installed, first in School House where I lived with my family, and later in my classroom, where all calls, including highly sensitive ones, were monitored by 20 small children, all seemingly engrossed in their studies, but with all 40 ears focused on the conversation. It was at a later date, when extensions (including an office with a telephone) were built, and when incoming calls resulted in numerous interruptions to my teaching, that I recalled, wistfully, the time when the telephone had been safely at the other end of the village.

These extensions became necessary when a considerable building programme in the village resulted in a sharp increase in the number on the roll. Tarrant Gunville School was due to close, the children being relocated to Pimperne together with their headmaster, Mr Vic Willmott. It took a year for the building work to be completed and the conditions under which the staff had to work were practically impossible. Outside walls were knocked down, canvas screens were erected and the noise was almost intolerable. However, we now had a new classroom, an extension to the main teaching area, a 'quiet area', an administration block comprising an office/staffroom, a staff lavatory and a kitchen.

The increase in school population to about 140 necessitated an enlargement in staff numbers. We had six classes, and three new teachers including a deputy head were appointed. Kitchen staff, a cook-in-charge with a kitchen assistant meant that we were able to produce meals for about 120 children on the premises, and excellent meals they were too. Hitherto meals had been brought from Blandford and they were good but nothing could compare with this 'home' cooking. It is amusing to read that the first cooked meals were brought to school on 11 June 1945, but by 13 July these meals were being blamed for a 'mysterious sickness'. In 1955 'a whole container of cooked peas were returned as the smell was vile and the peas like bullets'.

It was at this time that the constitution of the Governors was changed. Previously they had been known as 'Managers'. The Board of Managers in 1965 included the Revd Foxhall Smedley, Rector of Pimperne, Mr Edward Woodhouse, Chairman of Hall & Woodhouse Brewery, Brigadier Hanmer, Mr Michael Wilson, solicitor, and Mr A.B.C. Davis, a local farmer. They saw their function as one of leaving the headmaster to run the school whilst being prepared to justify his decisions when asked to do so at Managers' meetings. The new Board of Governors included elected representative teaching staff and parents and their role was vastly different.

The curriculum of the Infants' School established in 1827 included reading and the eldest girls were taught needlework. Later, in the National Schools, all pupils were instructed in reading, writing and arithmetic (the three Rs as we know them today). All 46 girls were taught needlework and knitting and 12 of the boys gardening. From 1918 onwards there were frequent mentions of curriculum in the logbook.

There were regular inspections by His/Her Majesty's Inspectors (HMIs) - shades of OFSTED today. There were tests and examinations, the scholarship and the eleven-plus. In 1918 'the girls' needlework was inspected and prizes given'. Later it was noted that the reading was fluent while written composition was only fairly satisfactory: 'some children are slow in mental calculation while written exercises in arithmetic are fairly good'. History and geography of the British Isles were studied, the older boys also receiving instruction in geometrical and scale drawing. Gardening figured largely in the activities for boys, while, in 1935, girls were 'interested in the cultivation of flowers'. 'Domestic subjects, including woodwork and gardening were taught by specialist teachers. The ages of the children in the top class were very different from today. In 1929 there were two children of 14, ten of 13 and seven of 12.

At the time of my appointment in 1965 the curriculum was still largely based on the three Rs. However, certain innovations were beginning to appear; for example, 'colour factor', a box of coloured blocks of wood, was proving very popular as an aid to mathematics. This had been introduced before my arrival and appeared such a success that Mrs Waterman and her class were often asked to give demonstration lessons for visiting teachers.

THE VILLAGE SCHOOL

In fact, this was but the beginning of a radical reorganisation of primary education. During the sixties and seventies great pressure was brought to bear on primary schools to make fundamental changes to their organisation and methods. Teachers who had, for most of their professional lives, based their work on a more formal approach were now told that this was wrong. We were told that a more flexible arrangement was to be encouraged. Timetables were to be abolished, and the 'integrated day' and open-plan classrooms became the aim. 'New Mathematics', mathematics workshops, and 'Do You Understand?' were watchwords. New reading schemes based on strange symbols were to be encouraged. Heads and assistants were expected to attend numerous courses and conferences to experience and evaluate these new methods and applications. Of course, some reacted enthusiastically, but many more felt threatened and breakdowns were common. Many eminent educationalists disagreed violently with the new theories. They published the 'Black Papers', denouncing the disintegration of the education system. Some pupils responded to the practical approach. Two lads, after a lesson on surveys, decided to hold their own. One lay on the pavement at the side of the road, the other hid in the hedge intending to count how many cars stopped to investigate – results not known!

It is interesting to note how music has always played a most important part in the life and curriculum of the school. As far back as 1918 the headmaster reported taking the infants for singing and later that year 'for singing and marching'. A year later one of the HMIs made comment that:

> ... the children [had] been trained to sing fairly well, but by the more regular practice of voice training exercises it [was thought] possible to avoid the necessity of almost completely suppressing the boys' voices!

In 1929 the senior pupils competed in a singing competition in Blandford and won a cup. They repeated this success in 1930 and 1932. Later HMIs commented that: 'music [was] taught very successfully as shown by the fact that the school [did] consistently well in local competitive festivals'. Singing and instrumental teaching, particularly on the recorder, continue to this day. Children from the school visit and play at the Weymouth Festival regularly. The present Head Teacher, Mrs Ann Cunniffe, noted that one

Top: *Celia Gilbert with the recorder group at the Weymouth Festival in 1989. Left to right, back: Paul Wynn, Katherine Gilbert, Josie Watson, Sarah Wentworth; front: Kerry Bright, Laura Shephard.*
Above: *Celia Gilbert with the School Choir at the Weymouth Music Festival.*
Left to right, back: Jessica Goodfield, Hamish Hogg, Alex Fowler, Ben Krauss, Samantha Cooper, Celia Gilbert, Hannah ?, Charlotte Bulpitt, ? Heaton, Kim Cornelius, Tom Randles;
middle: Hayley Froud, Sophie Johnson, Lisa Scott, Sean Gardiner, ?, ?, Ben Leigh, Clive Coats, Imogen Phelps, ?, Gemma Lacey, Graham Jenner;
front: William Bosworth, Sophie Wilson, Alexandra Brown, Lucy Percival, ?, Claire Barrett, Rebecca Manson, Jacqueline Powell, Charlotte Adams, James ?, ?, Darren Davies.

Right: *Nativity play, 1997.*
Below: *Nativity play in the church, 1998.*

of these occasions was indeed 'a wonderful performance'. However, the instrumental performance has not always been received in such an enthusiastic manner. Violin teaching was introduced in the 1970s, instruction being given by peripatetic teachers and on the first occasion when they were included in the Carol Service one very unkind comment was overheard – 'excruciating'.

It has been a tradition that has lasted up to the present day that Pimperne School has filled the church to capacity for its nativity play and Christmas music. It is the one occasion of the year when the whole school community can meet together; Governors, parents, friends, children and teachers. Through the years the school has had a close relationship with the church. The incumbent has always visited the school to take assembly, to teach religious instruction, to make social calls or, as is recorded in the logbook, to 'inspect the registers'. He was often the Chairman of Governors. The first mention to this effect was made on 16 January 1918, when 'the Revd Wilkinson visited'. The school was regularly inspected by the Diocese and on one occasion the Diocesan Inspector recorded 'the general tone and discipline of the school' to be 'good throughout', and at a later date, in 1940, the children to be 'well grounded in the sacramental part of the catechism'. In 1954, when Mr W. Lumb was headmaster:

... the effect of the Headmaster's personality and influence [was] noticeable... the children [were] well-mannered, polite, obedient and well-spoken to a degree unusual in rural schools.

Half-holidays were often granted for religious festivals, Ascension Day among them. They were also granted for royal events, including weddings and funerals. There were regular holidays given for Empire Day. Many entries in the logbook echoed those of 1945 when the children were given 'a talk about Empire Day [and] sang three national songs after which they marched into the playground and saluted the flag'. Although the logbook opened in 1917 little mention was made of the First World War apart from the admission of some soldiers' children to the school. However, in 1938 sites for children's trenches were chosen and the staff had to attend ARP (Air Raid Precautions) lectures. September 1939 saw an extra week's holiday 'on account of the outbreak of war'. In 1940, 28 evacuees from Southampton were admitted, although two days later two of them returned to Southampton. One member of staff left to join the WAAF (Women's Auxiliary Air Force), and in 1943 children helped with potato planting and later in the year with potato picking.

One of my first official functions was to open the swimming pool, one of the first such facilities to be built at a primary school in Dorset. It was a joint venture organised by the school, parents and villagers and it was to remain open for over 20 years. It was used during the summer months by the children of the school, by children from other schools and by properly organised and supervised family and village groups during out-of-school hours and at weekends. It was declared open by my predecessor, Mr Ken

THE VILLAGE SCHOOL

Drayton, who had overseen and co-ordinated the project from the outset.

Before the opening, however, it was necessary to fill the pool, and the only way was through a half-inch hose connected to a tap. That first night I was greatly concerned about leaving the hose on over night in case the pool overflowed. In the event it took ten days and nights to fill! Equally, no investigation had been made into the method of emptying 15 000 gallons of water from the pool. There was an old cesspit on site and it was decided to use that. Unfortunately, the capacity of the cesspit was 1000 gallons! A bewildered neighbour was appalled to see what appeared to be a fountain of water shooting out from the top of his garden and a wall of water heading down towards his house. The pump was rapidly switched off and other methods sought.

The swimming pool was a tremendous asset to the school. Very soon almost every child was able to swim and the building of the pool fostered a tremendous feeling of community spirit, so many different people from all sections of the village, many of them unconnected to the school, involving themselves in the project. I was fortunate enough to inherit this community feeling which stood the school in good stead later when, with the formation of a Parents' Association, we organised fund-raising activities.

The idea for the formation of a Parents' Association and for the adoption of a school uniform was born during a country dance display by the children for their parents one summer evening in 1966. A group of parents commented on how smart the children looked, particularly the boys, most of whom wore similar clothes; white shirts and grey trousers. The idea for a uniform was floated and such was the enthusiasm that a referendum was held, not only about a uniform but also about the formation of a Parents' Association. The result for a uniform was overwhelming, for a PA less so, many expressing reservations that a few strong characters might dictate policy. In spite of this we pressed ahead with both. The Managers also had reservations about a uniform; having to a man been educated in the private sector, they felt that blazers, caps and pinafore dresses might prove too expensive for many parents. They were reassured, however, when it was explained to them that more simple, inexpensive items of clothing were envisaged. In the event almost all parents adopted the uniform for their children.

Parents' meetings were usually well attended. This was particularly so at the time of the 'new education' and the Black Papers when feelings were running high. Parents, teachers and Governors were invited to attend to discuss and evaluate these new ideas. Exchanges were both intelligent and reasoned. Many meetings were held over the years to discuss such widely differing topics as the teaching of French in primary schools and the desirability of sex education for very young children. That we were able to expect such good attendances was due almost entirely to a strong supportive Parents' Association.

The enthusiasm of successive PA committees knew no bounds. Meetings were a pleasure, always amicable and often hilarious. November Fayres were the principal money-raising activities and were very well supported, especially when the sky-diving Father Christmas landed on the school field. There was one occasion when his main parachute failed to open. We watched in horror but fortunately his auxiliary shute opened and he landed safely in the garden of a house in the village, much to the surprise of the occupants!

I must admit to having had one or two sleepless nights caused by PA events when we lived in School House. The first bonfire party was held on the school field, the bonfire lasting well into the early hours. Would it spread to neighbouring houses? Of course not, but I did get up to check once or twice during the night. On another occasion a parent, a farmer, brought a number of hay bales into school one Friday in preparation for a barn dance on Saturday. A fire hazard? Of course not, but I did get up to make sure.

The school has always enjoyed the support of the local community and there was no better illustration of this when, in 1986, the BBC invited schools to take part in a Domesday project, 900 years after the original Domesday Book was compiled. Pimperne School elected to take part and many local people gave liberally of their time, none more so than Mrs Jean Coull and the late Mr Jack Antell who worked with the children over a long period and whose knowledge of the locality was of immense help.

As a start survey forms were distributed around the village and about three-quarters were returned giving a picture of life in the community, its work and play. The children interviewed local residents, Mr Fred Waterman, Chairman of the Parish Council, explained the workings of the Council and Mr Peter Boyt compared farming today with the situation as he remembered it when he had started 14 years previously. Mr D.W. Taylor told how his family had started the industry, Taymix, and Mrs Helen House talked about her husband's business, O. & J. House, Landscapers and Computers. The Adjutant from Blandford Camp, from whence many Pimperne pupils came and where many of their parents worked, spoke of the Royal Corps of Signals, its history and its role in the Army of today. There was also great interest in the great Workings of Steam, or as it is more popularly known, the Steam Rally, which is held annually, a celebration of the days of steam-driven machines which has become famous worldwide.

A Year 2 foursome at playtime: Lottie Flanagan, Amy Peat, Clare Bartlett and Sophie Mogridge.

Two pupils were inspired to write poems for the survey, the first, Richard Hunter, wrote about the magnificent horse chestnut tree near the church:

> *The Horse Chestnut tree*
> *Is a tree full of delights.*
> *It is a big, beautiful tree.*
> *It has many wonders,*
> *Why was it planted outside the church?*
> *How old it is, how big is its spread,*
> *What it has seen in its long, long life.*
> *It has seen a party under its branches this year*
> *To remember victory in Europe forty years ago.*
> *In the summer it has luscious green leaves;*
> *In autumn the leaves are a lovely red, golden yellow brown.*
> *They fall and crunch under your feet,*
> *Then comes the conker with its hard, spiky shell.*

The second, by Amy Watson, tells of the threat to flora and fauna:

> *Will they die;*
> *The beautiful, shy roe deer,*
> *as it darts through the undergrowth,*
> *pretty and sure footed?*
> *The snuffling, busy hedgehog, pushing through the bushes?*
> *The badgers, sometimes half asleep, sometimes bustling,*
> *eating earthworms, woodlice, slugs?*
> *The hopping rabbits, running briskly over fields?*
> *Lovely plants, the soft-mauve scabious,*
> *the bright yellow of lady's bed of straw,*
> *the tiny purple and yellow of the*
> *woody night shade? And so many more,*
> *beautiful butterflies, tortoiseshell.*
> *The graceful movement and lovely colours of the peacock.*
> *Will our sprays and pollution kill them?*

I have many memories of my time at Pimperne, most of them happy ones, but one tragic event will remain with me as indeed it will with all who were in school at this time. In 1974 an infant child, Jacqueline Secretan, died of meningitis. There is nothing more distressing than the death of a young child and in a small community school, such an event perhaps seems so much more personal. We felt very close to the parents both of whom had always been actively involved in the school and tireless workers for the Parents' Association. Imagine our concern when, two months later, another child contracted meningitis; thankfully it was a different strain and he survived...

Happily, so many more pleasant memories remain. Christmas activities were always great fun, particularly the Carol Service. Our self-contained kitchen enabled us to invite friends, County Hall officers and Governors to join the school for Christmas lunch as a way of saying 'thank you' for their support. The school dining room looked a picture set out as it was with the tables laid so attractively.

Then there were the pageants performed on the Rectory lawn during the Village Fête. All of the costumes were made by the parents and I recall one lad, acting the part of Henry VIII, complaining that his getup was causing him great discomfort. We put it down to stage fright until we realised that it was, in fact, made from fibreglass.

For a number of years we joined other schools in the Blandford area and took a group of children to France. Their introduction to 'unisex' lavatories caused some consternation – the bidet too – and there was a certain apprehension when confronted with a plate of 'moules' for the first time. One return ferry crossing was made during a rather severe gale and many were seasick, one in particular, but he had a very good friend who cheerfully disposed of his 'bags', counting as he went – he reached double figures, if my memory serves me correctly.

Then there were the many visitors and events which enriched the lives and experiences of all of us... the music advisors who frequently gave concerts using a variety of instruments, ancient and modern... our participation in the Blandford Music Week when the children joined groups from the Bournemouth Symphony Orchestra to make music... our own musical afternoons when the children entertained parents and friends with programmes of singing and music making... and the more relaxed days of years ago when we could afford the money and the time to close the school and take every child and many parents in three coaches on annual educational/social trips to Bath and Bristol Zoo, Longleat, the New Forest and Christchurch. There were swimming galas, country dance afternoons, 'the fastest sports days on record' and school photographs when Mr Ekhardt, the local photographer, in an endeavour to make every child smile, so excited them that he caused chaos, then left us to quieten a school full of highly-charged children... but the photographs were excellent!

Yes, so many happy memories. Finally, 19 December 1986 saw my resignation recorded in the logbook. I had been the sixth Head Teacher at Pimperne School since 1917.

Roll of Headteachers

Mr W. Fry	1917-1927
Mrs G.E. Fuge	1927-1945
Mrs E.G. Wells	1945-1951
Mr M. Lumb	1951-1954
Mr K. Drayton	1954-1965
Mr D.M. Reed	1965-1986
Mrs A. Cunniffe	1986-2000
Mrs C. Rimmer	2000-

Mrs Ann Cunniffe succeeded Malcolm Reed as headteacher in January 1987. While coping with an ever increasing load of paperwork, computer technology and the demands of OFSTED, she has kept the school a happy place for children to learn about the modern world.

Over the years she has enjoyed the wholehearted support of an excellent staff. There has also been a good friendly involvement between teachers and parents, with the PTA organising annual spring events and November Fayres. Mrs Cunniffe retired in August 2000, and took with her our thanks for all her hard work over the years in making Pimperne such a happy and successful school and our best wishes for the future. In the middle of her busy last term, she found time to sum up her years as headmistress:

During almost 14 years I have witnessed several changes to the school curriculum and to the building. The terrapin classroom, which was used for storage when I first began my headship, is now fully restored as a classroom. For the second year in succession we have a class for each year group, making five classes in total. Long may that be so!

A further development of the school building came in the shape of a wonderful new hall, albeit a mobile construction. The hall was erected in the summer of 1997 and was handed over to the school in September. It has proved to be an extremely valuable resource even though it meant filling in the school swimming pool, which by then was in dire need of repair and there was not the same need since the opening of the Blandford Leisure Centre swimming pool.

Many wonderful children and staff have passed through the school during my headship. The following photographs illustrate some of the school's activities and achievements in recent years.

The Village School
by Barbara Ellis

In careful copperplate the master kept
A daily record of the village school.
It was smaller then, seventy-two on roll,
And the two oldest boys nearly fourteen.
Children of the village and the farms absent in summer,
Harvesting the hay; absent in winter
When heavy rain or snow made the long walk impossible;
Pleasing the Church Inspectors with
'A very reverential attitude in Morning Prayers.'
The journal chronicles the small events
Which punctuated the syntax of the year;
'It being Ash Wednesday the school attended
Morning Service in the Parish Church.'
In June, on Empire Day, the school assembled,
Sang patriotic songs, listened to speeches,
Silent and shuffling, waiting patiently
Until the half-day's holiday was announced.
In summer through the drowsy afternoons
The boys worked in the garden, taking
A week to lift the school's potato crop.
The master's notes are short, laconic even,
'The School Attendance Officer came today,'
'Today the Rector instructed Standard Four'
Then suddenly a brief aside reveals the man:
'Today I took the infants for music and drill,
The children sang most sweetly.'

Other headmasters follow, other hands –
But still the continuity of routine persists.
The Rector makes his regular weekly visit;
Wartime comes and goes, scarcely remarked.
The older pupils leave for schools in town.
Buses collect the bonny children now
From neighbouring villages, whose decline is marked
By the closure of their schools.
My children came here too, when they were young;
They and their fellows all have gone
Like fledglings from the nest, to work elsewhere.
And still the school endures, enlarged, adapted,
Suited to present needs, fitting the children to live
In a larger world than parish and local town.
Nightly the present headmaster opens the Log
And choosing his words with care
Commits the passing day to history.

DOWN THROUGH THE YEARS: 1935–1952

Above: *Pimperne School Football Team, 1938, in Arlecks Lane. Left to right, back: B. Dacombe, T. Dacombe, L. Joyce; front: L. Riggs, G. Reglar, ? Rigler, R. Joyce.*

Right: *Young prospective cricketers in 1938 (in the field which later became St Peter's Close). Left to right, back: B. Dacombe, L. Joyce; front: T. Bamlett, R. Joyce.*

Pimperne Church of England School, 1935. Left to right, back: Frances Rigg, David Hawkins, Len Vincent, John Ridout, Audrey Fletcher, Betty Attwool, Pat Arthurs, Rosamund Davis, Kath Riggs, Joan Hawkings, Bobby Head, Walter Cuff; front: Mary Rose, ?, ?, Tommy Bamlett, ?, Edith Turpin, Cyril Randall, Joan Hunt, Leonard Hawkins, Edith Arthurs, Muriel Davis, Bertie Daniells.

THE VILLAGE SCHOOL

The village school, 1949, with the headmistress Miss Wells on the right and the Revd Foxhall Smedley and Mrs Thornton.

The village school in 1952 with the headmaster Mr Lumb and Miss Pam Trickey (now Mrs Poole). Left to right, back: ?, Janet Taylor, ?, ?, ?, Mervyn Wells, Margaret Bennett, ?, Leslie Langdown, Barry Barnett, Tony Mundy, ?, ?, ?, Kenny Sturmey; 4th row: Keith Lucas, ?, Richard North, Billy Ellis, Johny Banks, ?, Anne Hull, Joan White, ?, Mary Hall; 3rd row: ?, ?, Bill White, Basil Pridmore, Clare North, Pam Trickey, Mr Lumb, ?, ?, Jackie Hunt; 2nd row: ?, ?, ?, Yvonne Henderson, Beth Langdown, Elizabeth Milbrook, ?, Gordon Maidment, Bryan Brett, ?, Wayne Wills, Billy Bavington; front: includes ? White, Jane Wells and Maria Wills.

THE BOOK OF PIMPERNE

Down Through the Years: 1960–1987

Above: *Pageant in the Rectory garden, 1968. Left to right: Julie Williams, Hilary Archer, Rosalyn Kaile, ?, Marion O'Donagh, Julie Hinchcliffe, Elizabeth Reed, Barbara Maidment, ?, ?; front, kneeling: Geoff Coull.*

Below: *The village school, Christmas 1961.*

Opening of the school swimming pool in 1964. Left to right, back: Mr Hayfield, Norman Pollard, Fred Waterman, Mr Bradshaw, A.B.C. Davis, Ken Drayton, Malcolm Reed, Edward Woodhouse, Mrs Davis, Muriel Reed, Michael Wilson, Mrs A. Langdown; front: Catherine Brett, ?, Marian McDonagh, Jenny Wilkes, ?, ?, ?, ?, ?, ?, ?, ?.

48

THE VILLAGE SCHOOL

Malcolm Reed with his last class in 1986.
Left to right, back: Malcolm Reed, Philip Morrel, Zoe Gent, Ben James, Matthew Parker, Jonathan Wynn, David Smith, Peter Hammond, Richard Drane;
middle: Elizabeth Bracher, Elizabeth Hughes, Helen Croft, Victoria Craddock, Christian Webster;
front: Millie Stanley, James Jones, Alison White, Claire Howland, Christopher Jelby, Christopher Osmond, Vicky Eaton, Alfie Talman.

Mrs Anne Cunniffe with her first class in 1986/7.
Left to right, back: Jamie Banks, Richard White, Amy Warwick, Simon Black, ?, Tim Davies, Alison White, Anne Cunniffe;
middle: Alfie Tolman, Charles Hunter, Andrew Reynolds, Mathew Bellman, Kay Vacher, Vicky Eaton, Claire Tanner, Melanie Pratt, Abigail Belbin, Daniel Torrence, Kelly Drennan;
front: Lynsey Gale, Daniel Quay, Tristan Craddock, Catherine Speakman, Ben Blake, Claire Bailey, Simon Maidment, Darren Pierrepont, Tim Ireland.

Turn of the Century

Left: *Year 1 in the gym in the new hall. Picture includes: Joanna Kennedy, Charlie Lacey, Jessica Knight, Tilly Bull, Rowan Reynolds, ?, Lewis Rowland.*

Right: *Reception class. Left to right, back: Rebecca Shepherd, Holly Elford, Grace Tory, Ethan Netherton, Michael Riglar, Ryan Foot, Rachel Howarth, Ellie Clements; on floor: Jade Brown, Hannah Evans, Sam Smith, Maisy Bull, Ben Kimber.*

Year 2 - what a line up! Left to right: Sophie Moggridge, Heather Bates, Emma Stroud, Claire Bartlett, Peter Wall, Cameron Hogg, Anthony Morris, James King, Jasmin Powell, Lottie Miller, Kirsty Wheeler, Georgina Towler, Michael Deakin, Katie Newman, Sam Burlton, Louis Glover, Alistair Williams, Owain Hughes, Eddie Sherbrook, Emily Brown, Amy Peat, Leanne Peaty, Nicole Tait.

THE VILLAGE SCHOOL

Year 3 hard at work, September 1999. Facing the camera are Alexander Francis, Alice Thomson, Melissa Foot, Bronwen Hughes, Leah Knight and Rebecca Hubble.

Year 4 at work. Back table left: Patrick Clements, Elizabeth Ebury, Verity Mackenzie, Laura Kitchen; back table right: Bryony MacMenemy, Martin Jenner, Aimee Collins; front: ?, Joshua Robinson.

THE BOOK OF PIMPERNE

SPECIAL EVENTS

Above: *Red Nose Day in the Village Hall, 1998.*

Above right: *Father Christmas arrives by parachute, 1983.*

Right: *Year 4 Clothes Show - the latest fashions using bin liners, designed and created by the children in technology lessons, 1996.*

Left: *Sports day and the look of a winner, Clara Powell.*

Below: *Sports days are such fun, but will the weather hold? July, 1998.*

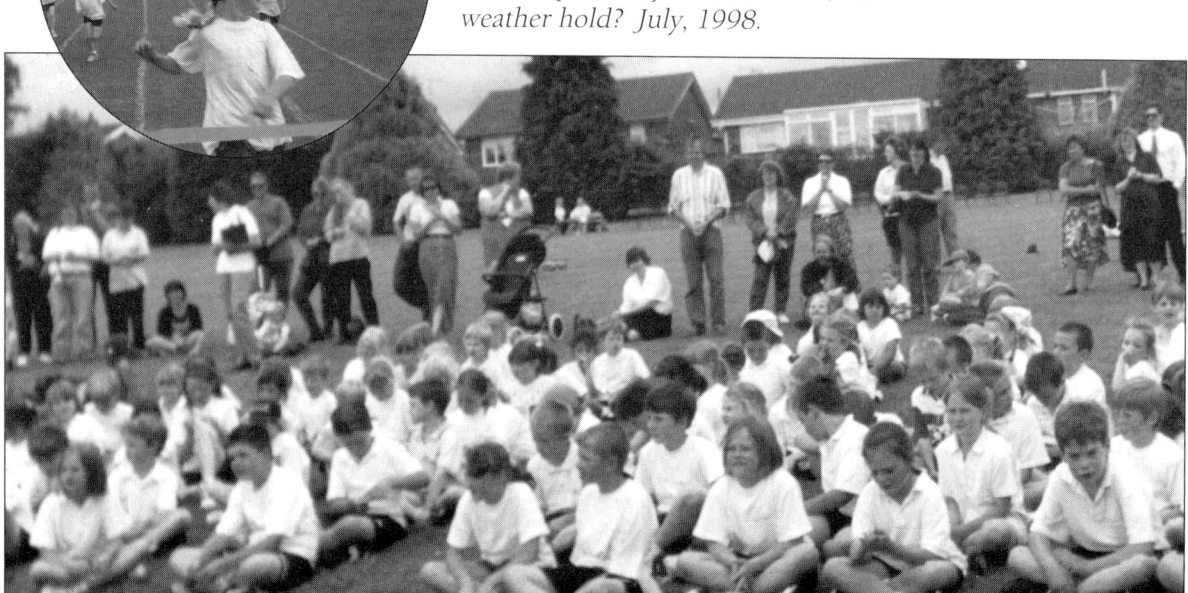

THE VILLAGE SCHOOL

Right: *Improving the environment. Jessica Goodfield holds the tree steady as Rachel Shemilt, Hannah Powell Bailey and Edward Saunders look on.*

Below: *With Nigel Mansell's Garage in the village in the 1990s Father Christmas arrived by Ferrari!*

Below, left: *Book Week, 1998 – a visiting drama teacher engages the whole school on the topic of dragons.*

Above: *Jack Antell and Sue Miles with schoolchildren at the top of the church tower on the Domesday project, July 1985. Left to right, back: Henry Almond Smith, Helen Cross, Rachel Cross, Sallyann Plumley, ?, ?, ?, Sue Miles, Jack Antell; in front: Ben ?, Zoe Gent, Clare Howland.*

Left: *'Hands on' experience as part of a project on 'Homes'.*

53

Kim Elliot, John ? and David Taylor haymaking with an Arbor Stationary Baler, Collingwood Field, 1950.

Weighing pigs in weaner pens c.1960. Joe Lynch, Nigel Trent, Ronnie Champion.

Chapter 5
Farms and Farming Families

with Michael Taylor, David William Taylor and Arthur Legge

At the beginning of the 20th century there was little to indicate the seismic changes that awaited the farming community. Virtually the entire village was owned by Viscount Portman and almost every villager was a tenant and/or worked on the estate.

The sale of the estates in 1924 in the parishes of Pimperne, Stourpaine, Shillingstone, Manston, Motcombe, Gillingham and Stour Provost must have sent a shockwave throughout the neighbourhood as land and property became available for purchase for the first time. The particulars give an interesting picture of farming at that time; there were ten farms in the parish varying in size from Manor Farm (630 acres plus 101 acres of woodland) to Berkeley Farm (131 acres). Every farm had an array of substantial farmhouses and buildings typical of mixed agriculture. A few along Salisbury Road had mains water, but most had wells and earth closets. The smallest farm had two cottages for workers, the largest ten.

Each farm had its cows, sheep, pigs and chickens as well as fields planted for hay and corn. Animal and water power, once prime movers on the farm, were augmented by steam traction engines for haulage, ploughing and threshing. For many years now, a taste of yesterday has been provided locally each autumn at the Great Dorset Steam Fair.

Water meadows were still in use on Manor Farm in the 1920s - an unusual agricultural feature, found mostly around the chalk streams of Hampshire, Wiltshire and Dorset. The flooding of water meadows in winter and early spring was controlled by a system of channels and wooden hatches. While depositing some fertile silt, this process protected the land from frost and gave an early crop of grass in the spring when grazing on the downland was still poor.

Milk produced on Berkeley Farm by R.J. and E.H. Old was retailed around the village by Clement Newbury.

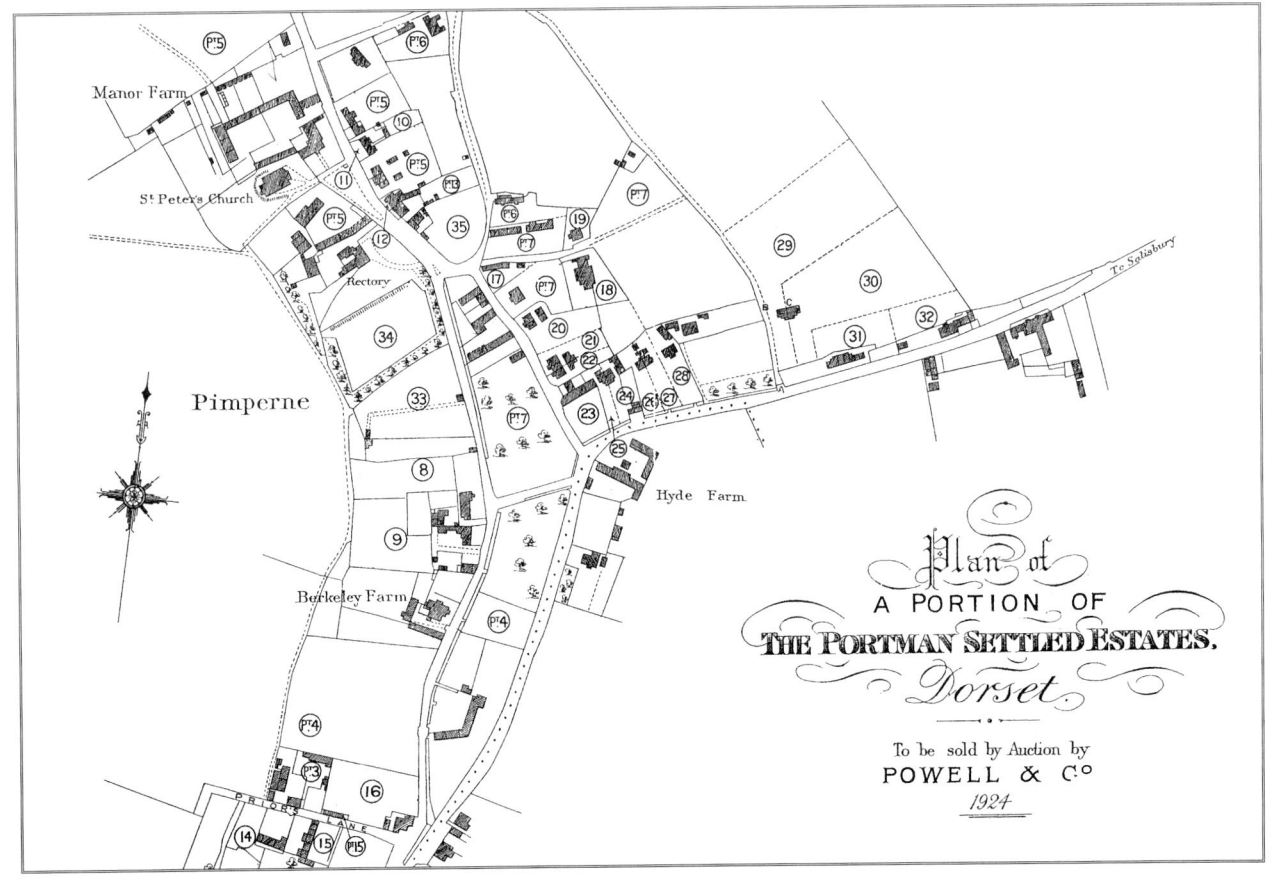

Great Dorset Steam Fair

Thrashing and baling. This method was used from 1900-1940s.

Above: *Fowler 8n.h.p. Traction Engine, No.8635. Year 1899, Reg.I B5747. It was new to a haulage contractor in Co. Down, N. Ireland, where it spent its life delivering goods around Newry. It lay in a wood for 50 years before being recovered in 1982 by its present owner, B. O'Gorman of Naas, Co. Kildare, and restored.*

Centre right: *Foden Steam Bus. Series No. 11340 Puffin Billy. Reg. No. M6359. Built in 1922, it was used as a brewer's dray before being sold to a Southampton showman and used on fairgrounds.*

Above: *Shires drawing a cultivator.*

FARMS AND FARMING FAMILIES

THE COATS FAMILY

The Coats family have farmed Hyde Farm since 1916. Before that they had a hay and straw business in Blandford, the premises of which were sold to the Post Office in 1929 and now house Blandford Post Office. The deeds of Hyde Farm date back to 1676, although the original house burnt down and was rebuilt in the 1890s. Building was interrupted by the Boer War and although the game larder was fitted with slate slabs and cupboards, the china room next to it had a dirt floor and the kitchen walls were not even plastered until 1963! There is a well in the farmyard where the old house was, but nothing is left of the house itself. There were springs all along the road and to get into Hyde Farm in those days one had to cross a little bridge over the stream.

The Coats family have always specialised in hay and straw. The long-stemmed wheat straw used for thatching was tied in bundles by hand until the 1930s by Alfie Wells and his father. Hard hay (a special mix including clover, ryegrass and sanfoin) was grown for horses, soft meadow hay was used for cows and calves and very soft downland hay was used until the 1950s to pack Poole Pottery!

Chas. Coats' father always kept horses (and these always greys) – even long after most other people had changed to tractors. Before pick-up balers arrived, there was a stationary baler on the farm and all the hay was swept into the rick and then baled from there. Wheatcorn was kept in ricks until 1965 because there was a substantial demand for thatching materials. Two lorries were kept for delivering corn and at that time a dozen people were employed on the farm whereas today Tim Coats farms with the help of just one man.

Above: *Haymaking at Hyde Farm in the 1950s.*
Below: *Aerial view of Hyde Farm, c.1970.*

DORSET.

In the Parishes of Pimperne, Stourpaine, Shillingstone, Manston, Motcombe, Gillingham and Stour Provost.

A PORTION OF THE

PORTMAN SETTLED ESTATES

Situate in the Northern Division of Dorset, chiefly adjoining the main Bournemouth to Bath Line of the Southern Railway; near the Market Towns of Blandford, Sturminster Newton and Shaftesbury; extending to about

4,340 Acres,

AND INCLUDING WELL-KNOWN

Dairy and Sheep Farms,

RANGING FROM 50 TO 700 ACRES.

SMALL HOLDINGS.   SPORTING PROPERTY.

RESIDENCES.

THE VILLAGE OF PIMPERNE.

BUILDING, GRAZING AND ACCOMMODATION LAND.

COTTAGES, SHOPS, &c.

To be Sold by Auction in 87 Lots, unless previously Sold, by

POWELL & CO.

AT

THE CORN EXCHANGE, BLANDFORD,

On FRIDAY, 30th MAY, 1924, at 2 p.m

Particulars, Plans and Conditions of Sale from—

Solicitors:

Messrs. GREENFIELD & CRACKNALL,
1, Clements Inn, Strand, London, W.C. 2.
(Vendor's Solicitors).

Messrs. WILDE, WIGSTON & SAPTE,
21, College Hill, London, E.C. 4.

Land Agent:
R. VERNON, Esq.,
Estate Office, Bryanston, Blandford.

Auctioneers:
Messrs. POWELL & CO.,
The Estate Offices, Lewes, Sussex.

FARMS AND FARMING FAMILIES

Above: *A Coats family wedding, photograph taken at Old Rectory, 1936. Included are: Mrs C. Coats, Mr Lethbridge, Mr Coats, Mr Richards (bridegroom), Miss Doris Coats (bride), Mr Richards (best man) and Mrs Richards senr. The three young bridesmaids were the Misses Arscott, cousins of the bride.*

Left: *Charles Coats (left) served six and a half years in the Dorset Yeomanry during the Second World War.*

THE DAVIS FAMILY

The Davis family bought Cemetery Farm at the time of the Portman Sale. It was farmed for many years by A.B.C. Davis (*right*), who was succeeded later by his daughter Muriel until her death in 1999. Both served for many years on the Parish Council.

Another member of the family bought Manor Farm (*below*) from the Taylors at the end of the war and built the new Manor Farmhouse.

Left: *Brick-and-flint buildings at Manor Farm, c.1980. The sale particulars for the farm from the 1924 sale list the buildings in the main block: '4-bay Cart Lodge, with Loft over; a range comprising Traphouse; Garage; Carthorse Stable for 6 with Fodder Space and Granary over whole; a range comprising Carthorse Stable for 9, with Fodder Room and 8-Bay Open Lodge, with Loft over whole; large 3-Division Barn, with wood floor and Loft over; Carthorse Stable for 2; Nag Stable for 4, with Loose Box, Fodder and Harness Rooms; Three Large Store Houses'.*

NEWFIELD FARM.

A Compact Hill Farm in a Ring Fence.
ABOUT 542 ACRES.

Approached by good roads and capable of carrying a large flock.

THE FARMHOUSE is at present occupied as two cottages. It is brick built, with slated roof. As occupied, Tenement 1 contains:—Entrance Porch; Sitting Room; Kitchen; Scullery; Four Bedrooms. Tenement 2 contains:—Living Room; Kitchen; Two Bedrooms; Three Attic Bedrooms. As a Farmhouse it would include Two Sitting Rooms and Five Bedrooms. Outside is Wash-house; Cellars; &c. Good Well of Water, soft water supply with pump. South aspect.

There are SEVEN COTTAGES as follows:—

Adjoining the Farm Buildings: A pair, brick and flint built and slated, each containing Parlour; Kitchen; Larder; Wash-house; Three Bedrooms; Outside E.C.'s and Pigstyes; Good Gardens.

In Pimperne Village: A newly-built pair capable, should the owner prefer to live in the Village, of being converted into a Farmhouse. They comprise: No. 1, Two Sitting Rooms; Kitchen; Scullery, with sink (h. & c. water); Larder; Three Bedrooms, one fitted bath (h. & c. water); Box Room; Outside W.C. No. 2: Parlour; Kitchen; Scullery, with sink and tap; Larder; Coal-house; Three Bedrooms; Outside Wood-house and E.C. A pair, Nos. 25 and 26, brick built, with slate roofs, each containing: Kitchen; Scullery; Three Bedrooms Outside Wash and Wood-houses and E.C.; Large lean-to Shed; Well of water. A single cottage, No. 23, brick, cement faced and thatched, containing: Kitchen; Scullery and Two Bedrooms; Outside Wood-house and E.C.; Well of Water.

THE FARM BUILDINGS include, flint built and tiled, 8-Bay Open Cattle Lodge in good yard; brick and flint built and tiled Root and Fodder-house, with 8-Stall Cow-house and Cattle-box adjoining; Waggon Lodge; Large Barn, with concrete floor; Cart Lodge, with Granary over; Brick, flint and tiled Cart-horse Stable for Six, with Fodder Room and Loft over; Brick, flint and tiled Open Lodge; Timber-built Store Shed and Chicken-house. Adjoining is a large Concrete Pond, to which the rain water from all buildings is conducted.

FARMS AND FARMING FAMILIES

D. Dalton and Son

D. Dalton and son bought Manor Farm from Davis in 1966. In 1971 there was a dairy herd of 80 Friesians on Manor Farm - today there are 160 cows taken care of by the same number of people; corn yields too have more than doubled. Peter Boyt has been farm manager for most of this time. All in all the Dalton family farm 2500 acres at Pimperne, Shaftesbury, Verwood and Bransgore, including three Manor Farms.

In 1983 Newfield Farm was purchased from the Lodge brothers. Sheep were run on the farm for three years, after which time marrowfat peas for human consumption were grown.

Top right: *Sale particulars for Manor Farm, 1924.*

Above: *Plan of Manor Farm showing the field names.*

Right: *Peter and Valerie Boyt outside the church at their son's wedding to Samantha Green, June 1993.*

Opposite top: *Sale particulars for Newfield Farm, 1924.*

Opposite bottom: *Newfield Farm, 1995.*

Coloured Blue on Plans 1 and 3.

STUDHOUSE FARM,
COMPRISING

Modern Farmhouse, Four Cottages, Buildings
And 157 Acres.

Situate with long frontage to the Blandford—Salisbury Main Road, and being only about 2½-miles from the former town.

THE FARMHOUSE is substantially built of brick with slate roof, and contains Tiled Entrance Hall; Dining Room; Drawing Room; Breakfast Room; Kitchen, fitted range and sink (with h. & c. water); Four Bedrooms; Bath Room (h. & c. water); W.C. Outside Wash-house, with soft water pump and copper; Coal-house; Wood-house and outside E.C.

The Water Supply is from a Well, from which it is pumped to tanks in the roof. Good Garden.

THE COTTAGES are conveniently situated near the house and are in two pairs. Nos. 27 and 28 are cement rendered and have slate roofs. No. 27 contains Kitchen; Scullery; Two Bedrooms. Outside Wash-house, Fuel-house and E.C. No. 28 contains Kitchen; Pantry and Three Bedrooms. Outside Wash-house, Fuel-house and E.C. Nos. 29 and 30 are brick built with slate roofs. No. 29 contains Sitting Room; Kitchen; Scullery and Three Bedrooms. Outside Wash-house, Coal-house and E.C. No. 30 contains Kitchen; Pantry and Two Bedrooms. Outside Wash-house and E.C. Company's Water.

THE BUILDINGS include a brick built and tiled Dairy, with stone floor and slate shelves; Meal House, with furnace and pump to Well; Brick, timber and tiled Trap-house; Timber built on dwarf brick walls and corrugated iron roofed 3-Bay Cart Lodge and Poultry House; Large flint built and thatched Barn; Carthorse Stable for 3 and Root House; Brick and timber built Carthorse Stable for 5, with Harness Room and Trap-house; Three brick built Pigstys; Brick built with corrugated iron roof (felt under) Cowhouse for 10 and Large Loose Box; Timber built Cart Lodge. In addition to the supply from the Well water is laid on from the main.

Sale particulars for Studhouse Farm, 1924, and an aerial view of the farm, c.1950.

FARMS AND FARMING FAMILIES

THE LUKINS FAMILY

The Lukins family came to Pimperne from Wedmore in Somerset in 1947 when Albert Lukins bought Stud Farm (now Bowmoor House) from the Taylors. At that time there was one tractor as well as three or four horses. He moved the dairy from the old buildings opposite the house (where the village shop is now) to the top of Down Road. An old First World War building was used for cow stalls (which is still there) and then a new unit for 25 cows (all milked by hand at that time) was built. Later the milking parlour was put in and cow stalls followed; here 60 Shorthorns were milked at first and later Jerseys and Friesians (the cream content was important in those days) which won prizes at many local shows.

Despite this success, poultry was always Albert Lukins' main interest. Eggs had previously been incubated in 150 egg units but he introduced a 12 000-egg-capacity unit which worked on a three-weekly cycle. He had electricity installed especially with a back-up generator. The chicken-breeding unit went from strength to strength, at its peak employing over 30 people including a geneticist. Breeding stock were sent all over the country, birds fetching ten guineas each (£10.50) – a lot of money in the 1950s and more than a week's pay for a farmworker. Although fowl pest came to the village the farm escaped and it was not until the general demise in poultry farming that the unit closed.

When Albert Lukins retired his son Austin carried on with the dairy side while John ran the poultry. About 36 people worked on the farm at its peak with the hatchery as well as three full-time dairymen; today Austin's son Alan runs the farm with only one assistant.

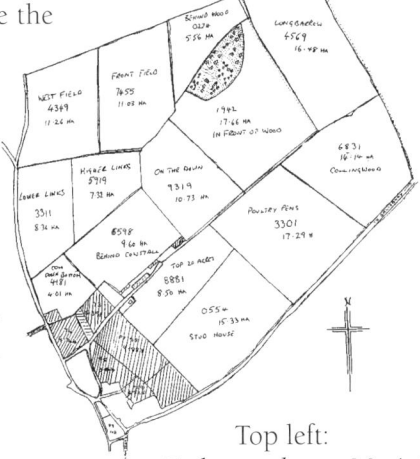

Top left: *Father and son, Mr A.G. Lukins and Mr Austin Lukins, from* Farm & Country, *February, 1958.*

Top right: *Four generations of Lukins: George Lukins holding Gordon, with his grandson Austin and son Albert behind at Rectory Cottage, Church Road, 1952.*

Above left: *Barbara Legge (Morris), Arthur James, Pearl Vincent (James), 1950s.*

Above: *Field plan of Stud Farm.*

Left: *Chestnut Farmhouse, which was converted into a home for Mr Austin Lukins, from* Farm & Country, *February, 1958.*

63

THE BOOK OF PIMPERNE

Main picture: *Reg Joyce and Austin Lukins silo making in the 1950s.*
Inset: *Austin and Evelyn Lukins with son Alan and his wife Julie, 1993.*

Main picture: *Chicken houses, 1957/58.*
Inset: *More intensive poultry keeping – John Lukins, c.1970.*

FARMS AND FARMING FAMILIES

THE TAYLOR FAMILY

The Taylor family have farmed in Pimperne since the 1870s under vastly changing circumstances. Arthur Legge, born in 1900, tells of his life as a shepherd on Manor Farm, recalling that at that time there were 25-30 men and 34 horses on the farm which covered over 2000 acres.

David Taylor was 18 in 1939 when he left school and went straight to Sandhurst. A captain in the Royal Tank Regt, he was in the Secret Service and a prisoner of war, and worked sending messages for which he was awarded the MBE. On his return to Pimperne he found that much of the farm had been sold, only 123 acres remaining. He gradually built the holding back up, starting with a herd of pedigree Friesians and going on to farm about 1000 acres, with a large shoot. A very large intensive pig enterprise was also developed and he invented the Taymix Sturdymixer liquid-feeding system to cope with the thousands of animals he kept.

The Taymix Transport company formed in 1959 now operates across the whole of the United Kingdom delivering washings from yoghurt, ice-cream, jam and milk factories to modern versions of the Sturdymixer, with experts advising farmers on the precise ratio of ingredients their pigs need. From small beginnings the company grew until, in 1999, it ran 32 trucks and had a 45-strong staff, including four Taylor family members.

David Taylor's sons carry on the business, Michael farming, while Rory owns Taymix Transport and his son Robert now operates his own transport business - Taylor Distribution Services. Robert is the fifth generation of the Taylor family at Pimperne.

Above: *David Taylor swath turning, Collingwood Field, 1950.*
Below: *The pig unit at Yarde Farm c.1960.*

Taymix Ltd.

Left and bottom left: *Taymix Mill, 1960s and map of the farm.*

Below: *The 1960s and Taymix were increasing the number of different vehicles to transport their products, from large flat trailers to transport straw to long-distance lorries for carrying pig meal.*

Bottom right: *Taymix Mill, c.1970s (now Old Bakery Close).*

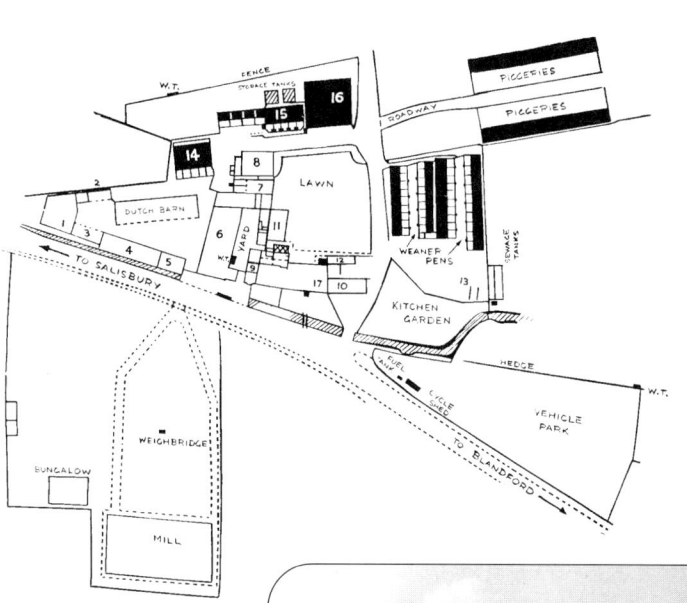

1 Fitters Shop
2 Tractor Shed
3 Tractor Shed
4 Whey and Meal Mixers
5 Grinders
6 Farrowing Crates
7 Long Sty
8 New House Piggeries
9 Office
10 Garages
11 Fruit Cage
12 Garage
13 Cattle Body Stand
14 Old House Piggery
15 Piggery
16 Barn Piggery
17 Long House
W.T. Water Trough

FARMS AND FARMING FAMILIES

Today Michael Taylor farms Hammetts, Nutford and Langton Lodge Farms. In an interview during May 2000 he recalled how farming had changed:

We farm 1200 acres plus contract work and we have got one employee now. It's hard to compare, because of differing turnovers and methods, but when my father started he would probably have had five employees on 250 acres. In the 1960s you would have done well to produce two tons an acre; we are now up to four tons. It is very good, and that is a lot of the problem - farmers have produced so much that it has flooded the market.

We have been through quite a revolution in recent years because everything we sell has dropped in price, some of it by as much as 50 per cent. For instance, the price for wheat off the combine this coming harvest is about £58 a ton; five years ago top-quality milling wheat would have fetched £120. This means you have to be more efficient to stay still and the only way you can do that is by producing more per man and cutting overheads and costs.

I'm lucky really because I can remember the thrashing machines going round when I was very young, thrashing the ricks. My father had a self-propelled combine, one of the very first ones, and that was a 6ft cut and it would cut about ten acres a day. The one we have now has a 20-foot cut and it will cut 120 acres a day. Farm work has become more automated and less physical. For instance, we will start work in the morning and get on a tractor which has an air-conditioned cab, air seat, heater and radio and it's quiet - real luxury to drive, but you do 14 hours on it non-stop - it's quite lonely (but I have got a telephone and computer in it).

If I bought the combine new now it would cost £100 000 and the tractors £50 000 each. Smaller things like the sprayer would be £20 000 and they are all electronic, even the tractors have got little computers in them. The combine has a lot of technology and gadgetry too, to help the driver; it stays level on hills and that sort of thing - the old combines were pretty basic. The days when you could take farm implements to the village blacksmith for repair are long gone and I can see the next stage coming when repairs will be done on the farm with parts obtained direct from the manufacturer via the internet; I think the dealer will go.

There is EEC-subsidised Set Aside, where you have to have 15 per cent set aside to grow nothing or a non-food crop, for instance linseed, which is used for making lino and linseed oil; we do a bit of that but it involves a lot of paperwork.

BSE has caused the whole farming industry the most terrific upset; we had about 35 cases. The politicians wouldn't face it and once they did they went to town on it - they made it cost everyone an awful lot of money and the French and Germans have taken advantage of our serious approach to the problem in order to stop all of our beef going there for such a long time. It has crucified our beef industry and it will take a great deal of time to recover - perhaps as long as 20 years.

We have always had pigs but we sold the last in 1998 when prices went right down and we could not keep going. We had two dairies and the same thing applied; we were getting 24 pence per gallon of milk and now they are getting 13 pence - it has paid us to get out.

We have a shoot; Nutford Farm has got a lovely valley that makes for high pheasants and my boys are very keen on it. We grow a bit of kale there and put the pheasants in that; it's quite a low-key thing and very enjoyable. At one time the shoot was enormous and it was a big headache. Both William and Thomas are keen to go to agricultural college at the moment and I think that they will farm, but you never know. I am only a caretaker really, I have to hand it over to them in as good a condition as possible. I took it over with that in mind and this is what the townies don't understand; you become very attached to the land, you can't stop living for it. Our relaxation is the shoot, but if you ask me what I would like to do in my spare time, I would say farming!

Top: *Haymaking, 1950.*
Above: *Two Claeys M103 combines making a 12-foot cut in Sunnyside, Yarde Farm, 1960s.*

Cottages between the Parish Room and Reading Room, Church Road.

Mr Taylor's Talbot outside Reeves' shop and bakery, 1920s.

FARMS AND FARMING FAMILIES

David Taylor wrote his memoirs in the 1980s, the early chapters of which recreate his childhood days in the village in the 1920s and '30s and we are indebted to the Taylor family for allowing them to be reproduced here. Together with Arthur Legge's account of his life as a shepherd on the same farm at the same time, they present a fascinating and authentic picture of a way of life on the farm and in the village that has all but disappeared.

Arthur Legge (*left, c.1940*) was a shepherd, born in the village in 1900. His father and his grandfather were both shepherds for the Taylors at Manor Farm, Pimperne, and Arthur tells how he left school at 12 to join them. His future wife (below) came to Blandford Camp with the Air Corps during the First World War and was billeted with his family. A widower at the time of the interview in 1985, Arthur was living in an old people's bungalow in Portman Road, cooked his own meals and kept himself and his home spick and span. Although diabetic and rather lame, he enjoyed being driven around the countryside, visiting his daughter and her husband in the Midlands and took a keen interest in the village darts and cricket teams. He recalled:

I was born in the cottage next to the Parish Room (one of three, opposite) and moved to the other end when we were married. I left school before I was 13; Mr Taylor signed a paper and took me away from school when I was just gone 12 - you could do that in those days.

I went on the sheep with Father, he showed me what to do although I knowed more or less 'cause I was always up there at weekends along with Father. Before I were born Father and his brother used to walk down to Nutford (about three miles), shear some sheep and walk back by six o'clock in the morning. I used to go all over the place shearing along with Father, never walked, they used to come and pick us up at five o'clock. We used to do all the work and shear all our own sheep - that were about 1500 sheep.

Father was a shepherd all his life, he had certificates for sheep shearing and thatching and all sorts. Lambing was the busiest time, that was 24-hour call, that was. We had 300 lambs in three days, Father called I on the Saturday morning, every man on the farm were there, on Sunday too. Mr Taylor used to have 25-30 men on Manor

Arthur's future wife, Beatrice Bennett (*seated fourth from the left*) at Blandford Camp, 1916/7. Also in the picture are Betty Barnard (*standing third from left*) and Bessie Amy (*seated second from left*).

Right: *Arthur and Beatrice Legge, 1950s.*

Below: *Barbara Legge, Bridge View, 1940s, at the age of 7. She left school at 14 and worked at Lukins Hatchery until she married Bill Morris, who was serving in R.E.M.E. at Blandford Camp (in 1957). They moved to Sutton Coldfield.*

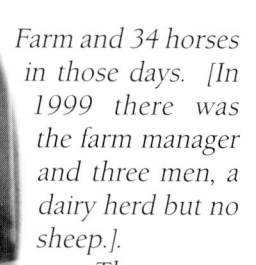

Farm and 34 horses in those days. [In 1999 there was the farm manager and three men, a dairy herd but no sheep.].

There were thousands of sheep at the July Sheep Fair in Blandford. Used to have to walk them, they would drive 300 or 400 to the other side of Salisbury. We mostly had two dogs each, trained them ourselves. We had some good dogs, you only had to go into the field, put your hand like that there, and he did know what to do. We had one big dog and Billy Taylor said 'Don't you ever get rid of that dog Jim' (he called Father Jim) - 'He is worth a groundful of men!' To train a dog you would run with it yourself for a bit, then let it run with an older dog; some we used to chain on to the other dog to keep them there.

I got £1 a week when I was married and I got a two shilling rise just after. I got a lot of overtime; that were twopence an hour then. I suppose I can say what a lot of people can't say, I had more money than I should have had all my life; I asked for more pay and I got it. I mind the first time I was harvesting. I was about 19 and that were man's work then. I came home to Mother and said 'I am going to ask for more money tomorrow and if not, I am going in the Army.' 'Oh no, no!' said Mother. 'Yes, I am', I said. Next morning I said to Mr Taylor 'I want a word with you please.' 'Oh, what's the matter Art?' he said. 'Nothing's the matter, nothing whatsoever, only I think I am doing man's work and I am entitled to man's pay.' 'You shall have it Art.' No hesitating. He were very good. Oh I suppose I mu'n say I was hurted all the time, you got your pay and you didn't worry about the work you done.

I might have an afternoon off on Sunday if Father didn't want to go anywhere; if Father wanted to go I couldn't. I mind the first holiday I had. It was after I were married. We were harvesting, I said to Mr Taylor on the Thursday 'Will we have finished harvesting tomorrow Guv'nor?' 'I got a bet on it Art, what you want to know for?' I said I wondered if I could go away for the weekend, he said 'What's stopping you?' and I went away on the Saturday morning and came back on the Tuesday. He paid I for the three days. We went to the wife's mother in Leamington, that were a good place - next door to the pub - it's all knocked down now.

Mr Taylor had the first car in Pimperne, we got a ride in it too! There were three of us outside the shop I mind, 'You boys like a ride?' 'Cor yes, yes, yes!' 'Go and tell your mothers where you are going then.' Up we goes, it was one of those with a little dickie seat and a canvas hood, he never had the hood up. I've seen as many as seven or eight up in that car - with prongs in their hands!

I have done everything under the sun on the farm. I went on the sheep with Father until the 1914 war, then Mr Taylor sold some of the sheep and I took on the horses. Horses were best I think, although with the sheep you were more or less your own boss. With the horses we used to start at four-thirty or five, feed the horses, then back for breakfast at six o'clock. We used to work until three o'clock. As long as you done your horses it didn't matter what time you got out there, but you always had to go out to the stables in the winter time at seven-thirty or eight in the evening and if you had a bad horse you had to stop out there all night. You didn't know when the boss would walk round. When I were thatching I used to get up early in the morning, specially when it was hot, I used to prefer it a bit damp for thatching - when it were dry you had a devil of a job.

Just after the First World War, Mr Richards was rector, he sent up home one day 'Tell Arthur and his intended to come and see me.' We went on down there, we was talking to him, he gave us a piece of beef and a tea set. We had some very good parsons. There were about 54 or 56 houses in Pimperne then and I knew everyone in the village - I don't now. The main road to Salisbury was not tarmac, it was made with stones. We used to walk into Blandford every Saturday to get your cheap stuff; the shops were open till near on ten o'clock at night. There was a butchers, Boseys, that was a nice shop in Salisbury Street - had the

FARMS AND FARMING FAMILIES

Left: *Manor farmyard from the church tower, 1985.*

Below: *Arthur Legge being presented with an award marking 50 years of membership with the Agricultural Workers Union by Jesse Waterman, County Secretary. Reg Joyce is on the left.*

Bottom: *Arthur Legge with two horses at Manor Farm.*

best of everything. We carried the shopping home on our backs.

Billy Taylor was very good, if he was there with his gun at night and you were along with him he would say 'You want a dinner Art?' 'Thank you!' 'When I stop,' he would say, 'You just walk on.' Always got a hare, I used to like em specially when they were cold, jugged, gravy and all that. I wouldn't eat a rabbit now. The best time to have a pheasant was on the nest - have the pheasant, eggs and all! Only once I ever sucked an egg in my life, Father he used to pick 'em up and suck them back all the time.

Mother was a very good cook. I mind the first dinner I cooked. Mother used to suffer these sick headaches, I had to stay home from school to cook the meal; what do you think I done? I put all the lot in one saucepan! Mother wasn't happy unless she had a houseful. Christmas time we used to have about four Christmases. Three or four uncles, all go to one house one day and the next house another day. My uncles who lived in Blandford used to come every other Sunday for dinner. We had to work on Sunday, not so much in the summer after dinner; then we would go off in the pony and trap. Roberts used to have a pony and trap to hire.

In the evenings we used to have dances, Mr Saint used to run the dancing class, sixpence a week. Mother used to run the whist drive every week. The Reading Room was used for billiards, you had to be there fairly early in the evening else you couldn't get a game. There were a lot of practical jokes. Some nights you would go out and your bike was gone. 'Where's the bike gone then?' You would find it up on top of the roof! They were good days.

71

THE BOOK OF PIMPERNE

Excerpt, by kind permission of Mrs Norah Taylor, from the Memoirs of David William Taylor, MBE, Pimperne 1921-1988:

Prologue

On June 1st 1867 my grandfather, Thomas Taylor, wrote the following letter to his sweetheart, at Pylle in Somerset, who in due course became his wife.

Montacute
June 1st 1867

Dearest Ann,
How I wish I was at Pylle, and that I was permitted to spend all my time in your sweet company and no more to be reserved as before not daring to speak my love for you, but to enjoy each other's company openly and open our hearts to each other.

Never shall I forget the last evening I spent with you, and the feelings I experienced. Dearest, I often fancy myself beside you. I pray that you may be my guiding star through this life and that I may be enabled to prove myself worthy of such a treasure. Mine is no shadowy love caused by what others might have said of your excellence, but a fixed affection caused by your warmth and loveableness in my own estimation.

I wish I had your carte de but I am happy to say your smiling face is before me most visibly. Dearest, do write and increase the happiness of thy impatient and most affectionate lover.

Thos. Taylor

On 16 December 1869 Thomas and Ann's first child, William, my father, was born. Within a year the family moved to Pimperne in North Dorset to take up the tenancy of Manor Farm on the Portman Estate. My grandfather died in 1901 and my father took over the running of the farm.

I was a mistake, born last and long after four daughters. I never really knew my father, who was 52 at the time. He was an arrogant and domineering but popular character, 6ft 3ins tall, tough, bearded, and with only one eye.

I slept in the dressing room next to my parents' bedroom. Lying there in the chill early hours I could hear my father return from the second of his twice-daily visits to the Crown Hotel in Blandford. He drank a bottle of whisky every weekday and two on Saturdays, the extra one to make up for Sundays when he drank nothing. Bracing myself for the eruption I knew would come, I pulled the bedclothes up over my head to try and block out the terrible sounds of my parents arguing. Father took little interest in me, and my welfare was left entirely in the hands of my mother. Sometimes, though, I would ride out round the farm with him, visiting each man where he was working.

As we rode, Father on his hunter, me on my pony, he would occasionally break the silence by firing sums at me, barking out figures and waiting in agitation for my response. Once he'd got the answer he wanted he would tell me to remember it. As a result I have always been good at mental arithmetic.

Other outings with Father included a regular Sunday-evening walk around the entire ten-mile perimeter of the farm to check the fencing for damage where rabbits could get through. He was fanatical about rabbits, going to any lengths to keep them off his land. He kept badgers specially for this purpose and even bought badgers from neighbouring farmers as they would kill hundreds of rabbits.

Thomas and Ann Taylor.

If we weren't riding or walking on the farm we would be travelling the fields at great speed in his old Talbot car, sometimes chasing a stray dog reported by the shepherd to be on the loose among the sheep. I had to steer while Father drove at break-neck speed holding the gun out over the side door to shoot the dog.

A similar routine was followed each year just before my grandmother's birthday, on which my father always provided a brace of golden plover for her favourite lunch. But it did mean a frantic pursuit in the Talbot across acres of arable with him screaming instructions at me to steer where he could get a shot at the birds.

I had all sorts of tasks to do around the farm as I got older, some for money but mostly just through duty. The catapult and the 16-bore shotgun that my parents had given me both played their part in some of these jobs, while other duties were performed through sheer hard physical work. I was taught to do three things in this order: feed the dog, clean the gun, wash yourself!

In time I was deemed old enough and responsible enough to go out shooting alone, and my

FARMS AND FARMING FAMILIES

income rose dramatically as a result of the hundreds of rabbits I shot and sold.

In the meantime, however, other uses were found for me on the farm. At lambing time, because my hands were much smaller than the shepherd's I had to pull the lambs out from the ewes that were having difficulty in giving birth. Lambs which had lost their mothers were fostered on to ewes which had lost their lambs. This was done by skinning the dead lambs and placing the skin over the orphaned lambs with its four legs through four holes in the corner of the skin, which it then wore as a kind of jacket. The new mother only accepted the orphaned lambs this way, as she smelt the skins of her dead lambs and thought they were her own.

At this time of year we lived on mutton from the ewes which died in lambing or which had been killed just in time to be bled. These were hung in the farmhouse cellar and then we and our relatives took all we needed. The remains, now too far gone for human consumption, were fed to the dogs. These periods were followed by eating the lambs' tails when they were docked and their testicles when they were castrated, so virtually nothing went to waste. The sheep were usually being fed or folded on roots or kale and sometimes, if the weather was hard and fresh greens scarce, I had to help pick the kale tops into bags for selling on to local greengrocers.

Once I ran home, refusing to do any more, and got a hiding with a cane. Father chased me across the garden and I had to jump a thick hedge to get away! The cane was kept behind the sideboard and Father never hesitated to use it if he felt I had misbehaved in the slightest way.

I was paid for catching rats on the farm. I would catch them in gin traps, cut off the last inch of their tails and put them in a tin. When I gave him the tin he would pay me a penny for each tail and then throw them in the fire.

In the winter I sometimes joined the men when they went out ferreting. The whole farm was systematically ferreted right over at regular intervals by two pairs of men working together.

Father paid me ten shillings a year for keeping the whole farm free of ragwort. It took many days to uproot by hand all the ragwort plants from every field and all the downland. He owned 2850 acres in all, of which well over 1000 were woodland or downland.

He kept a lot of sheep. That was about the only thing you could do in Dorset in the twenties, but as frozen 'Canterbury' lamb later began to be imported from New Zealand many sheep farmers faced ruin. Father forecast this and gradually changed to dairy cows. He set up three dairies and eventually a fourth. But it was the sheep, and in particular his two big flocks of Hampshire Downs, that interested him most.

During my father's farming life the Portman Estate was split up and sold. As somebody in the family died a farm would be sold off to pay the death duties. My father accumulated his acreage by buying up these farms one by one, saying he made his money from his activities on the Stock Exchange. At the same time he led my mother to believe he was penniless and seemed to keep her in torment on a mean housekeeping allowance.

In the early part of the 20th century Pimperne consisted of 30 or 40 thatched cottages either side of the Winterborne Stream or the road. At the higher end of the village were four large farms of 500-1000 acres each, being Manor Farm, Stud Farm, Newfield Farm and Paradise Farm. These were all owned by my father who worked them all as one unit. In addition he owned a small farm of 100-200 acres, Yarde Farm, at the bottom of the village. Here there were two other small farms, Berkeley Farm and Hyde Farm, each of about 150 acres, which were the only ones in the village my father did not farm.

On the road to Blandford were four more small farms, one of which was Damory Court Farm just a mile from the town. This was the home and headquarters of the Tory family and it was here that my mother was brought up.

Father loved gambling and trading and betting and regularly bought shiploads of Egyptian cotton cake for cattle feed which would be stored in barns on the farm. He would then sell this off later to his friends during the winter.

The only holiday my parents ever had was when they went to New Zealand travelling on the Mauritania and visiting Napier the day before the big earthquake. Father brought home with him a crate of 150 000 cigarettes bought in Panama on the homeward journey and there was a tremendous fuss at customs!

My maternal grandmother, Elizabeth Gale Tory, lived two miles away in Blandford and I had to visit her every day to give our news and deliver any surplus farm produce or vegetables and fruit from the garden. When I left for home I had to take a similar package for my mother consisting of food or items of clothing for which we might have a need. Surplus produce or any other items from every member of Grandmother Tory's large family were exchanged in this way. The family was so large that it was unnecessary to do much business outside. The system was even extended to swapping bulls, rams and seed corn.

It was all organised by Grandmother who, despite being bedridden, made absolutely certain that anyone who had more than they needed passed it on to other members of the family. This built up family strength economically and helped many of them to survive the slump.

The family gatherings at Grandmother's house at Christmas were enormous affairs. Several hundred of us would be there, divided into separate rooms for children, teenagers, parents and the senior members of the family. Games were organised all day.

My mother had eight brothers and sisters, three others having died in infancy. Her father had always said he would put every son into a 1000-acre farm and every daughter would marry a 1000-acre farmer. As a result of this extraordinary achievement the family farmed many thousands of acres locally, and whenever there was a family gathering about 200-300 of all ages would turn up.

Grandmother's house became my daily destination once I stopped having individual private tuition at the village school. I would ride to her house on my pony, leave it tethered in the old coach house, and then walk in to the kindergarten in Blandford. After school I returned, collected the pony and rode the two miles home.

Sometimes I was greeted on the outskirts of the village by the orphan lambs that I was rearing. They would get braver and braver and each day come further out from home to hurry me on my way so they could have their bottle of milk.

My sisters were away at boarding school, but occasionally Ruth would turn up at home having run away. She was always up to some mischief. She and I sometimes climbed up into the loft of the barn where we would smoke the Kensitas cigarettes she bought at the village shop. From our vantage point we could watch the bulls serving the cows out in the yard. Once Ruth found an old clay pipe and we took turns at smoking this until we were both sick. How we didn't set the farm buildings alight I will never know.

Although my father seemed tight with his money within the family, outside and in the village he was generous and always made sure the family as a whole exercised generosity in its dealings in Pimperne. To this end, Manor Farm became the sort of Social Security centre for the village. If anyone was sick we would send them food. Mother cooked a hot meal every day for expectant mothers and those who had just had babies so the husbands could continue working.

If a man hurt himself and had to stay at home, then it was our doctor who went to him. My mother had been trained as a nurse before the First World War when she had gone out to Italy during the War of Independence. I had the greatest faith in her as a nurse and she always appeared very confident.

Any scratch or wound had to be sucked or licked clean first, she insisted, and then iodine was poured on and followed by a hot poultice twice daily if required.

Among others I knew in the village were the blacksmith, who I often used to watch at work, and a little old spinster who lived in a tiny thatched cottage where she took in washing and mending and made lace. There were two small village shops, one a general store and the other a tobacconist/confectioner.

Nearby were the remains of Blandford Camp. The Royal Naval Division had been reviewed up on the downs at the top of the farm, when King George V had taken the salute standing on the Long Barrow. The whole division marched past him before they left for Gallipoli. About three-quarters of them were casualties after the landing and many of their wives, girlfriends and families were living at Blandford. When the casualties were made known the relatives walked sadly up from Blandford to the camp. Because of their attire the road they took is known to this day as Black Lane and at Collingwood Corner nearby there is a memorial to those who did not return from Gallipoli.

At one of my father's four dairies, Yarde Farm, there was a marvellous man called Pitman in charge. Father always said he was the best dairyman he ever had and the one who got the most milk out of the cows. Pitman and his wife and children milked 85 cows twice a day, by hand, for nearly 40 years with no holiday. I spent a lot of

Left and below: William Taylor in 1874 and 1879. He was the first child of Thomas and Ann Taylor and was born on 16 December 1869. At the age of one he moved with his parents to Manor Farm where he spent the rest of his childhood.

FARMS AND FARMING FAMILIES

time with Pitman. My father thought a great deal of him and he was so devoted to my father that he always put his duty before his family. Faced with the choice of going to my father's funeral or his own son's wedding when they fell on the same day, he opted without hesitation to honour my father.

We installed the first milking machine in the area but we had so much trouble with the cows getting mastitis, and trouble with the milk itself, that Father chucked it out after the first year and reverted to hand milking.

Sid Hunt worked for Father, driving the steam engine on threshing days. At about five he would stoke up the engine with coal and get up steam in time to give two blows on the whistle at six-thirty to warn the men he'd be setting off in half an hour. At five to seven he gave a single blow and finally, at seven, a long whistle gave the signal for work. Then he pulled a lever and the big driving wheel started slowly to pull on the long belt and, blowing out steam in all directions, thrashing would start with every man in the correct place doing his own particular job.

Yarde Farm had water meadows down below it and Sid was the drowner. This meant that he controlled the flow of water on the ditches when the stream came up in winter and spread it out over the grass, thus keeping the ground and the grass warm so the frost wouldn't burn it and it would grow very early in the spring. Then Sid would take up all the hatches and let the water go so that the cows could go out and eat this early grass a month or six weeks early in the spring.

Sometimes on Sunday afternoons I went with my father to see how it was progressing. It was wonderful to play with the water, sending it in different directions with little boards everywhere and pegs to hold them in slits cut in the ground. The water was controlled by the level of hatches everywhere. It seemed marvellous to me. Occasionally the cows after calving would get milk fever from feeding on this lush grass. To stop the milk flow and to save the calcium being exhausted from the system the teats would be blown up with a bicycle pump. Nowadays it's simply a matter of an injection.

When I was seven my mother had me vaccinated against smallpox, very much against my father's wishes. It was a new idea then and he said it was too risky. They argued for ages about whether it should be done. I had five huge marks on my left arm and then my temperature started to rise. I became so ill I nearly died. My anxious parents used to sit downstairs by the fire in the evenings with my father accusing my mother, 'I told you so, now you've killed him.' But she hadn't.

I had to kneel by my bed every night and say my prayers. I was taught to say certain things at certain times and on certain days of the week, always with the Lord's Prayer. In times of difficulty and trouble later on in my life I always found the habit easy to return to and it was possible to get strength from this on occasions when one was in dire trouble.

At a meal we always had to finish what we had taken or sit there until we did. We usually had rice pudding or sago or tapioca every day as a pudding with stewed fruit. In the kitchen was a huge bin with a sliding top. In one compartment was flour, in the next was rice, and in the third was tapioca, and these items were bought by the bag of 224lbs.

At the lower end of Pimperne was a baker, general store and Post Office called Reeves. Opposite was the village pub, the Farquharson Arms, where Mr Adam was the landlord. Some of the cottages had mud walls two feet thick, being a mixture of chalk and rye straw. Many others were flint and brick with slate roofs built by the Portman family, the original landlords of most of the village. The farmhouses were of similar design and each with its farm buildings was clustered in the hollow well below the level of the downs above.

There were three or four other houses in the village of superior design and size occupied by the more prosperous traders from Blandford. At the higher end of the village was the church of St Peter, on one side of which was the large Rectory within a big walled garden. On the other side of the church was the Manor House which my family occupied.

The smaller farms kept some cows in the lower meadows astride the stream. They also kept pigs and sometimes small flocks of sheep. At the higher end of the village the four large farms had two or three small fields of up to five acres adjacent to the farm buildings. Above these there were normally four or five large fields of between 50 and 100 acres abutting each other, so that at the bottom end they were next to the main farm road or track and at the top end they each adjoined a large area of downland which stretched from one side of the farm across the top to the other side. Sometimes this doubled or trebled the total acreage of the cultivated land and it was never ploughed. It consisted largely of indigenous wild grasses, clumps of gorse and abundant wildlife. There were of course many exceptions and variations to the basic farm layout. The four large fields were worked in a variation of the standard Norfolk four-course rotation which had been accepted farming practice for centuries. Most tenants were tied to this farming structure by their landlords, with such provisions as 'no two straw crops to be grown subsequently' and 'wheat only one year in eight'. The large flocks of Hampshire and Dorset Down sheep were folded with hurdles on one of about four fields at a time and exercised daily on the downland at the top where they nibbled on the selected herbs of their choice and dried their feet to ward off foot rot.

The road through Pimperne was the main road from the South Coast to Salisbury and London and was made mainly of packed flints picked off the chalk fields. Either side of this road above the villages the downs seemed to extend as far as the eye could see, with no hedges or fences but populated by wandering flocks of sheep and millions of rabbits.

My mother came to Pimperne from Damory with her own horse and trap as well as her own gardener and cook. When she married my father in 1911 they went to London for their honeymoon and there my father bought his first car. It was a Talbot four seater with a dickey and canvas hood. He drove this car for the rest of his life and it became famous in the district.

Manor Farmhouse was a large, L-shaped house with three entrances, as is traditional with farmhouses – a front door, back door and farm door. The front door was rarely opened except for ushering in important visitors, and if any tradesmen dared come to any door other than the back door they were reprimanded by my mother.

My father had control of the farm door. In the porch were coat pegs and a place for taking off rubber boots. The pegs were usually occupied by couples of rabbits or pheasants or other game, destined either as presents for outsiders or for our own kitchen. A variety of hats and caps hung there too, so that the right headgear was always easily accessible whatever the activity, be it riding, shooting or meeting some visitor.

Among the reception rooms the drawing room was the most important, with its large piano and the very best furniture. This room was only used on Sundays or for the reception of an 'outside' member of the family or important visitor or guest.

The dining room had an enormous table which had been handed down through the generations and which was used always for the two main meals of the day. At all other times the breakfast room was used where a fire was kept burning day and night throughout the winter.

The staff consisted of a resident cook who was assisted on many occasions by the wife of Harry Fletcher, the gardener, and two parlourmaids, one superior to the other, who served at table while the underling did all the dogsbody work. She had to scrub all the large area of flagstones which covered the floor of a huge kitchen, scullery and larder.

In the corner of the breakfast room was a small desk which contained my father's entire farm office operations. As far as I know this consisted solely of a cheque book, his latest bank statement and two enormous wire hooks in the shape of an 'S' which hung on a nail on the wall over the desk. Every invoice that came was placed on one of these and on payment day it was transferred to the other hook without any disturbance in the sequence. I gather it was common practice then to estimate one's profit or otherwise purely from your bank statement. More money in a year in there meant you had made money, and less, of course, meant the opposite.

Farmers in those days paid no tax if they filled in a form to say that their profit was less than the rentable value of the farm. If it was over the rentable value they paid a fixed tax based on the farm's rentable value, and therefore they had a great incentive to make money as they could keep it. But this was at a time when it was almost impossible to make money on a farm...

On the first floor of the farmhouse were four main bedrooms looking over the village, and behind these were three more looking over the farmyard. There was one general cloakroom downstairs and one lavatory and bathroom upstairs as well as yards and yards of passageways. Each of my sisters had a bedroom of her own. I always slept in the dressing room over the porch and next to my parents' bedroom. A very large bedroom at the back was converted into a bed/sitting room for my eldest sister. She was totally confined here in winter during the latter period of her life while she slowly died of lung TB. I was only allowed to stand in the doorway of her room and talk to her but her coughing could be heard in the background most of the time.

Another large room had been turned into a nursery and playroom for all of us children and for the use of our resident governess. After breakfast we had to go either up to this room or get out of the way on the farm. After lunch we all had to go to bed for an hour and then go for a walk on the farm. If it was wet we went to the playroom until it was time to go to bed.

On the next floor up, which was mainly attics, there were four more bedrooms. Up here the resident cook and parlourmaids had their quarters.

My father smoked continuously and my mother took exception to this and tried to confine his smoking to the breakfast room. On Sundays he would sit in a high chair by the fire in the breakfast room and read, finishing a book within the day. He was very knowledgeable about world affairs and educated himself a lot on matters about which his farming colleagues were quite ignorant. He used this knowledge to exploit the Stock Exchange and Monday mornings would usually find him on the phone to his stockbroker. He steadfastly refused to attend church.

He had brought the first telephones to Pimperne and had then refused absolutely to be put on the Tarrant Hinton exchange. Instead he paid £200 extra to be put on the Blandford exchange, as it was common knowledge that the woman who operated the Tarrant Hinton exchange listened in to everybody's conversations and knew all their business. People said that if you asked for a certain number she would be likely to say 'It's no good trying to ring them, they've gone to have supper with the So-and-Sos this evening, and won't be back until 10p.m.'

Our house was lit with oil lamps and at dusk one of the parlourmaids would light some of them, putting the large ones in the rooms that we would be using that evening and a row of smaller ones on a table ready for each member of the household to take one up to bed. The lamps were cleaned and maintained in a special lamp room, but in the 1930s we brought electricity to Pimperne. My father offered free installation to everybody who worked for us but if they refused the offer would not be repeated. Old Sid Hunt was one of those who declined, saying it was a new-fangled device that would set fire to his cottage and we would all soon be changing back to the old ways.

Each morning my father would get up at six and get dressed in the dressing room where I was supposed to be still asleep. His was a rough and speedy operation, not pausing to shave or wash, and he left in a collarless shirt to be out in the yard in time to meet all the men as they came to work at six-thirty. Most of the men were not due to start work until seven but they chose to arrive at least 15 or 20 minutes early so that they could chat with Father and he could talk with each one without being rushed. After giving them their orders for the day's work, my father would come back to the house at about seven-thirty and get washed, shaved and properly dressed. He usually wore breeches and below the knee of these was a long row of small buttons which had to be fastened in sequence. I was always fascinated by the speed with which he could do this without even looking.

Breakfast was at eight and was always three courses. A must at the start was porridge with either sugar, cream or salt, but never with more than one of these. This was usually followed by eggs and bacon and then toast and marmalade or toast and butter, but never all three.

Father bought a wireless in the early 1930s which was installed on the window sill of the breakfast room and he always listened to the eight o'clock news in the morning and the six o'clock news in the evening. Silence was the absolute rule for everybody in the room at those times, so that he could hear exactly what was said, particularly with regard to the weather report and news of the Stock Exchange and the main events around the world.

If we were in the breakfast room in the evenings there were two oil lamps, one for Father if he was there and positioned exactly so that he could read The Times from beginning to end before he left for the Crown Hotel in Blandford, and the other was in the middle of the table to be shared by everybody else who needed light for what they were doing.

William and Emily Taylor with son David and daughters Elizabeth, Rachel, Hannah and Ruth, c.1930.

On her marriage in 1911 my mother had brought with her from Damory Court in Blandford her personal gardener, Harry Fletcher, and his wife who would be her cook. They were both the most loyal of servants and neither of their families had ever worked for anybody else. Harry joined up in the First World War, as had many others of the farm staff, but he was wounded twice and badly gassed in the trenches. He survived and returned to continue as gardener. His wife was a most magnificent cook. Both were very hard working and I think my father thought even more of Harry than my mother did, for he was a gardener who was also willing to turn his hand to anything else on the farm. Harry looked after four or five horses, the car and a walled kitchen garden of an acre and a half.

At the top end of the farmyard was a big barn next to which was a large pond consisting of two feet of deep mud with six to twelve inches of water over the top from which the carthorses drank. Thus, on a hot day when they came in thirsty, the surface of the pond would be warm and they would not get chilled by over-drinking.

My father had five main carters who each looked after three enormous Shire or Belgian horses, and a dogsbody. Ernest Hunt, Sid Hunt's son, was considered to be a little soft in the head, and he filled the role of dogsbody. He did all manner of odd jobs with the horses and with a variety of carts and wagons. He was mainly involved in fetching and carrying for the flocks of sheep.

One day he arrived sweating and exhausted in the village pub at lunchtime. He wanted a pint of beer, quickly. 'What's the matter?' he was asked. 'Guv'nor told I to paint the mangold slicer, and I've spent nearly all morning with two ladders and planks trying to drag 'ee up into the tallet over the garage with a rope on me own, and by 'eck 'ee's 'eavy.' 'Whatever do you want to drag it up there for?' ''Cause that's where I keep the paint.'

The carters, like most others, worked a very long day, six days a week. At five o'clock in the morning they came to clean out, groom and feed the horses, removing the muck and dirty bedding from the back and moving the front bedding to the back so that none was wasted. They went home at six for half an hour for breakfast and then came back to harness the horses ready for a seven o'clock briefing from my father when he gave out instructions for the day.

I understood they always ate a cottage loaf of bread a day and a huge chunk of Cheddar cheese, and they sometimes came to work with the whole cottage loaf with the cheese inserted into a hole in the middle to keep it moist. They ate at least the whole of the top at ten o'clock with a bottle of cold tea or beer. They stopped work in the fields at three o'clock and rode their carthorses home, having walked from one end of the field to the other for eight hours almost non-stop. Then the horses were watered and fed after being unharnessed, and the carters were able to go home at five. At eight or nine in the evening the carters returned again to feed and bed down their horses for the night. They whistled to them until they urinated, not leaving until they had succeeded. Any sickness was then reported to the farmhouse, even the slightest thing wrong with any horse being considered serious enough to cause concern. This prompted the appearance of a beer bottle full of peculiar black physic that smelled foul and a long, strong stick with a slip knot at one end. The slip knot was put round the horse's upper lip which was fairly large and bore a moustache kept trimmed by the carter. This was then pushed up until the horse's nose touched the wooden roof of the shed and its jaw fell open. The contents of the bottle were then poured into the corner of its mouth and down its now vertical throat.

Norah Taylor presenting a tankard to Harry Fletcher in appreciation of 50 years service to three generations of the Taylor Family, May 1961. Harry started as a groom to Henry Tory in 1911.

When the horses came in from work in the summer the folds of skin above their hooves were searched systematically by the carter for maggots. These flicked out with the points of their penknives which they had earlier used to cut their bread and cheese. They pushed Stockholm tar in between the folds to discourage more blow flies and to heal the wounds.

Fletcher would normally bring my father's horse to the farm door of the house at nine o'clock, all ready and saddled for him. When I accompanied my father we went to visit all the teams of horses doing field work. He wanted to see that everything was going all right. I remember once visiting the ploughing team in a field when it must have been November 11th. At ten minutes to 11 the church bells could be heard in the village.

FARMS AND FARMING FAMILIES

At eleven o'clock they stopped, as did all the men and their horses, no matter where they were in the field. Everyone took off their caps. My father sat still on his horse with his cap in his hand. I believe the traffic stopped in Blandford... and people halted on the pavement. The First World War had not long been over and most people had lost... relatives.

Watching the ploughing, I saw that three horses usually pulled a two-furrow plough but on light, fallow land only two horses were used. On heavier fields two horses pulled a single-furrow plough. With virtually all the implements the horses walked a straight line from one end of the field to the other and seemed to know as much about what they had to do as the men in charge of them. Cultivators were the heaviest implements to pull, and then trace horses were fitted to the front of those hitched directly to the cultivator. The older, trained horses were always put on the outside and any young or new ones went in between two older ones. How we successfully farmed so many acres with just five main teams of working horses I find it difficult to understand, but it was done and done well, though the acreage actually cultivated compared to the whole was not great and the working of the land was not done very deep.

Horses do not damage the land as much as tractors and they can work in wetter weather and for more hours per day and more days per week than is accomplished nowadays.

The first two Fordson tractors were delivered in the early 1930s. They had steel wheels with spuds on and my father took on two extra men to drive them. They were hardly allowed to stop as the capital investment must have seemed excessive at the time and every bit of work was required to make it worthwhile.

A lot of what was grown on the farm was also used on the farm. There was at least one field of oats for the horses, the oats being crushed and the straw cut into chaff about an inch long and mixed with them. The wheat was sold for milling and the 'tailings' kept for feeding the farm chickens which ranged free in and around the farm buildings in large numbers as eggs were sold locally for cash. Wheat straw was used for thatch on the farm for all the ricks and cottages. A large acreage of kale and turnips was grown which the sheep folded off.

Lambing was in December/January and the lambs were sold off and sent to Smithfield for the early spring lamb trade which was profitable as it was the first fresh lamb available after the winter and it was mostly milk-fed. Huge steam-driven lorries arrived towing trailers with three or four decks on each to load the lambs. They frequently came on Sunday afternoons to be in London first thing Monday. The sheep and lambs were fussed over all winter in order to get those lambs off at the earliest possible date before anybody else's when they were at their most profitable and before the price slumped through over supply.

A crop of clover would usually be grown. Part of this was folded off by the sheep during the summer and part of it was cut for hay for feeding the sheep during the winter. There was also a crop of barley which was the main money spinner. It was sold for malting and the prime formula for malting barley in those days was that it should have been sown on ground that had been roots folded off by sheep. So a standard rotation would have been: roots (kale, turnips, etc.) folded off by sheep, sown to spring barley which was undersown to clover which was folded off by sheep or cut for hay and then sown for winter wheat or winter oats in the autumn for the following year, making the rotation turnips, barley, clover, wheat or oats. The cash crop was the malting barley, the wheat and the lambs. Everything else was fed on the farm.

There were many other things to be organised each day besides the arable. The shepherd was boss of all things and everybody seemed to be at his beck and call. Ernest Hunt spent most of his time hauling hurdles or water for the shepherd and the water had to be pumped by hand from a well in the farmyard into a horse-drawn water barrel.

Every day the shepherd and his assistant had to 'pitch' hurdles forward for the regular movement of the sheep. The lambs led the way through a creep hurdle followed by the milking ewes and then the stores and others who brought up the rear and cleaned up so that everything was manured over equally.

Old Sid Hunt, who drove the steam engine, also took charge of all the fencing, such as there was, and the installation, repair and renewal of gates. These were made, as were the wooden wagons, in the carpenter's shop by the carpenter, Ebeneezer, and his No. 2, Leonard Pitman. The carpenter's shop made and mended everything wooden on the farm.

There was a large area of woodland which was cropped in a regular fashion in rotation, the hazel being cut every few years to make hurdles. A man worked piecework on this and on the making of faggots for firelighting and beanstickers, which were sold, spars for thatching and fencing posts.

In the village lived Mr Cherry who owned a large outfitter's shop in Blandford, including a hairdressing salon and a china department. He was a very strict Quaker and noted for being straitlaced and for his adherence to high principles such as never indulging in drinking or smoking. Young Reg Legg was apprentice to the barber in Cherry's and heard my father come into the shop one day. Mr Cherry came up to him, 'Ah, Mr Taylor, I owe you for two bundles of faggots and three bundles of beansticks, how much?' 'Bottle of whisky,' my father replied. 'Oh sir, oh that's a bit difficult,' said the embarrassed Cherry. 'What, too dear?' 'No sir, oh no sir, no!' 'Well, too cheap then?' 'Oh no, no, no. I'll have one delivered to you tomorrow.' My father loved to pull his leg about his principles. Mr Cherry claimed never to have touched a bottle of whisky in his life, nor to have smoked and not even to have listened to the wireless.

The hedges on our farm were laid every 16-24 years, so that every year about one-twentieth of the length of the farm's hedges had to be laid and banked up from both sides with dirt after which they were stockproof. They were kept trimmed for eight years before they were allowed to start to grow away. They were virtually all blackthorn and very difficult to get through. It was a No. 1 offence to try and climb over a hedge as others would follow and this would lead to a gap developing.

The keeper, Ford, reared a lot of pheasants for a shoot which was let to a syndicate from Bournemouth, two guns being reserved for my father. Ford had a reputation for being able to call any bird to come to him and on Sunday afternoons many people from Bournemouth came out at an agreed time and met him at his cottage in Pimperne where they could ask to see a certain bird. Ford called it, and it came and settled in a nearby tree. Nowadays he would be famous for such a talent, but his skill was only locally known.

My father did not get on too well with his father's foreman, as is usual. The foreman said the reason why the wheat, when it was sown in the Old Kitchen Field, always got bunt, smut or rust, was that there was a barberry bush in the hedge. If he were allowed to cut it out, he said, the wheat would never again get diseased when grown there. My father refused to believe this and would not let him remove the bush. However, when the foreman dropped dead one day I was told that my father had the bush cut out immediately, so the poor foreman could never know that he was right. But he certainly was right, for it is well known now that barberry is the alternate host of this fungus disease which can reduce the yield of wheat by up to 50 per cent when spores are blown at the appropriate moment on the wheat flowers.

Rabbits were also one of the main crops and 10 000 or 20 000 were caught and sold every year. Four men were permanently employed in ferreting and catching rabbits in any way possible. Some of the downs were so thickly infested with them that they had eaten everything to the dirt near their burys and had to travel hundreds of yards to feed off neighbouring crops.

When these feeding rabbits were surprised on any occasion the whole surface of the ground seemed to move. They thrived on the dry soil of the chalk downs. The does could carry two litters at a time and a breeding pair could become 200 in a few months.

The first process in catching rabbits where there were a lot was long-netting. The next method to follow this was normally shooting at night with the aid of lights, or even just using sticks and dogs when the rabbits were dazzled by the lights. After that the rabbits would be snared and these could only be set in the runs well away from the burys as to get caught the rabbits need to be running fast. In my school holidays I kept 240 snares going. Following snaring the population of rabbits was kept down by ferreting. The ferrets were supposed to do a clean job, getting every last one, and so clearing up that area. However, it wasn't long before a 'clear' area was re-infested from neighbouring land.

One afternoon the well at Newfield Farm was being deepened and repaired so that the engine which drove the newly installed milking machine on the farm could pump water at the same time to a reservoir. My father had me lowered on a rope, sitting on a board, to the men working at the bottom so I could tell him what it was like. The well was 138 feet deep and when I reached the bottom I looked up to see if I could see the stars which I had been told would be possible, and I could. The hole at the top of the well now didn't seem big enough to get out of, appearing to be only about a quarter to half an inch across. It was an experience I would not repeat for anything.

The names of the four main fields were as follows: White Lane, being alongside a track which is now a road between Pimperne and Stourpaine; Path Field, which had a wide track in it leading up to a barn on the downs where the sheep were dipped to protect them from blowfly and maggots (the shearing, however, being done in a large building near the churchyard); the third field up was called Links and out in the middle of it in 1934 my father found the decayed carcass and bones of an enormous bird with, I believe, a 7ft wingspan. All the scientific experts around the district were called in to inspect the bird and many pictures of it were taken. It was eventually removed to a museum where it was declared to be an albatross.

I never heard it mentioned at the time but an albatross is supposed to bring bad luck to ships that it visits at sea. Within a matter of months of his discovery, my father died. The fourth field up

FARMS AND FARMING FAMILIES

was Old Kitchen, where the barberry bush grew in the hedge.

The men on the farm in Pimperne always forecast the weather and told the time by what they could hear from Blandford. In those days the countryside was very peaceful and quiet and when the wind was in the south west and... heavy with moisture as it was going to rain you could clearly hear every train going through Blandford, as well as the brewery hooter which sounded regularly.

On shooting days all the guns would normally arrive in cars but they would walk throughout the day. A horse and cart was used to carry the game and often surplus gear and cartridges as well as, occasionally, any guns who were getting a bit aged or decrepit and couldn't last the course. At lunchtime there would be a bonfire outside the keeper's house around which everyone stood eating their sandwiches.

Nearly all the guns wore plus-fours or breeches with leather boots and shoes and long stockings and garters or puttees, the latter left over from the First World War. I never remember seeing rubber boots. Since then, several farmers have said that the rubber boot was the invention of greatest benefit to agriculture - and I must say I agree.

The working men on the farm, carters and others, normally wore trousers tied with a piece of string below the knee so that it was very loose and baggy over the knee itself to enable free movement and prevent scratching and wearing the knee when bending especially in the wet. Men involved in work that necessitated kneeling, such as keepers and rabbiters, all had leather patches on their trouser knees.

The whole farm staff seemed to have heavy overcoats, obviously bought from Army surplus after the war. These overcoats would be worn in all weathers through the winter, until they were soaked. Then they were hung up to dry and a replacement taken from the ready supply on the peg.

The workmen's boots were all of very hard and heavy leather, shod with steel all around the edges and with many studs underneath. When I received my first pair I was so proud of my personal footprint that I left in the drying mud, my father having specially designed the pattern the studs should form. All the boots were made to measure in Blandford by a cobbler called Sherwood who became famous in the neighbourhood for the quality of his footwear. My father, though, never wore boots like the rest. His were specially made thick rubber-soled boots.

The whole family learnt to drive cars on the farm, there being no driving test and no L-plates. My father taught all my sisters on the downs. I was the first one to have to take a test - and I failed. I was fool enough to use my mother's new car which had a fierce clutch and I just could not start off on a hill without almost banging the examiner's head on the windscreen.

Harry Fletcher, the gardener, was a great friend of Harry Pitman, the dairyman at Yarde Farm. They formed a two-man darts team at the Farquharson Arms that was all-conquering in the district for many years. Both enjoyed a drink most evenings, when they could afford it. At one vital darts match it was Harry Pitman's throw and he had to get a double two for them to win. Harry Fletcher jokingly said 'I'll put my thumb over it. There you are, now let's see you put your dart straight through' - which is exactly what Harry Pitman did. Fletcher had to pull his impaled thumb off the dartboard - and they won again!

On another occasion, when they were in the pub on Christmas Eve, it was Fletcher's duty to switch on the lights in the church and ring the bells at quarter to twelve for the midnight service. He had had plenty to drink and only just made it home at eleven-thirty when he collapsed in the armchair. He woke suddenly from his sleep at quarter past twelve, pulled himself together and staggered over the road from the Brown House to the church. All the light switches were outside the entrance door. Harry swept his hand through the lot, thinking he was switching them all on, when in actual fact the congregation was all installed, and he was switching them off. He followed this by staggering up the steps to the tower where he started to ring the bell, right in the middle of the service!

Harry Fletcher is also remembered for the occasion when the vicar had forgotten to call the banns in the course of a series of announcements during a service. Harry shouted from the back of the church: 'Ere what about the banns? You've forgotten they!' With no other entertainment available the community thrived on little jokes and tales like these. In October one year, when the clocks are normally put back an hour, everyone told Harry Fletcher up at the pub that clocks were being put forward. Accordingly, on Sunday morning, Harry rang all the church bells two hours early and waited in his position at the back of the church for nobody to arrive!

From childhood I was brought up to believe Britain was boss. A quarter of the world was coloured red on the atlas and we had the biggest fleet with which to look after it. Living on an island made us invincible, I was told, and we could paint the other three-quarters red any day we wanted.

I was brought up with several basic loyalties: to my family, to my church, team, school or regiment and to my King and country.

THE BOOK OF PIMPERNE

Off to Sunday School in the 1960s. Left to right, back: Valerie Wilkes, Hilary Ellis, Janet Reglar, Marion Chinn; front: Julie Williams, Crispin Ellis, Rosalyn Kaile.

Pimperne Cubs formed a guard of honour at Peggy Coats' wedding in 1939. Left to right, back: Ken Reglar, Len Vincent, John Pike, Neville Poole, Reg Joyce, John Ridout, Bert Daniels; front: Arthur Ferrett, ? Stickley, Tommy Bamlett.

Chapter 6
St Peter's Church
by R.D. Allan MA

On 1 January 2000, a symbolic start was made to the new millennium when the seedling from a 2000-year old yew tree was planted at the top of the churchyard path. The parent tree has lived throughout the whole Christian era! Outside the porch of the church is another yew, of uncertain age but something approaching 1000 years old. Yews in churchyards - as every schoolchild knows - are there because, being poisonous to cattle, they must be grown in an enclosed space which the animals cannot reach, but, before the arrival of gunpowder, they were ideal for providing wood for bows.

'Pinpre', as the village was called in the Domesday Book of 1086, was already well established by that time and would have had its church on the site of the present one; this may well have been of wood, like so many other Anglo-Saxon churches. Whatever its style and composition, it was replaced in the 12th century by a stone church decent enough to last 700 years. By the 1870s, however, that church was in bad condition and was taken down three years later in 1873 by the patron of the living, Lord Portman. He was raised to a Viscountcy in the same year and it is interesting to speculate whether he was promoted because of his generosity in giving Pimperne a new church or whether the rebuilding may have been his way of giving thanks for the public honour.

Remnants of the Norman church survive incorporated into the new building. The Normans used a great many semi-circles and zigzags for decoration, and these may be seen in the chancel arch which was re-used on the north side of the choir. The doorway from the porch to the south aisle was inherited intact from the previous building. So was the font, although its handsome lid is more recent and is a 'Gothic' addition of an unusual kind.

The perpendicular tower is the earliest exterior part of the church and dates from the 15th century.

Pulpit and chancel arch.

As is usual it is stout and strong for the sake of stability when its bells are being rung. To this end, Lord Portman did nothing to it other than add battlements to its top, which have helped to keep a good proportion between the height of the tower and the ridge of the church roof. The extra weathering of the main part of the exterior reveals clearly where the additional course begins. The 12th-century church had been much smaller, and if you stand inside the present building at its centre and look towards the tower, you can see the marks on the stonework that reveal the lower height of the previous roof.

In the expectation that readers of this book may choose to use it as a guide when looking round, let us inspect the details of the church with some care. Lord Portman was clearly determined to provide a building of high quality, though oddly economical about the woodwork of the pews which are varnished pine of the plainest character. The cut and workmanship of all of the stone, however, are first class, with the finest mortar hardly visible between the blocks. The pillars of the nave are simple, but with rather elaborate capitals as was the 19th-century taste. The foliage is well carved but looks as if on the brink of exploding outwards. Above each is a slim Purbeck marble column, very appropriate for a Dorset church, rising to the roof and thereby giving visible punctuation to the bays.

On each side of the chancel arch there is a royal emblem; to the right the Tudor rose, to the left the portcullis of France, commemorating as usual the Tudor monarchy's claim to the kingdom of Aquitaine. The pulpit is of fine stone, medieval in style. The chancel is excellently finished in stone with neat panelled tracery around the walls inside the sanctuary, which is separated from the main area by a stone communion rail. There is therefore little need for many additional fixtures and furnishings. It seems a shame that there are no choir stalls or pews

THE BOOK OF PIMPERNE

The church in springtime with the yew trees on the left.

Steps behind the church leading to the burial ground.

remaining, but in these changed times Pimperne lacks church-going musicians in sufficient numbers to maintain a choir... and this in a building where Dame Clara Butt once gave a recital!

The most glorious and prominent stonework is at the east end. In 1868 the old church was provided with the magnificent large memorial window to the Wright family that had to be transferred to the new building. Few parish churches in Dorset have a window on such a large scale, and the splendour of this one dominates the church, especially in the mornings when the sun is streaming through it. Somebody once wisely said that to view Christianity from an unbeliever's position was like looking at stained glass from the outside. The religious minded person sees the faith from the inside, and can enjoy the brilliance of its light as through the Pimperne east window. Its panels illustrate the life of the church's patron saint, St Peter. The scenes broadly use the left side panels to describe four events in Peter's life before the Crucifixion, and on the right four more after the Resurrection, while the centrepiece is, of course, the crucified Christ, with St Peter beneath:

LEFT
a. Peter is called by Jesus – notice the beckoning hand.
b. Christ is blessing Peter at Caesarea Philippi.
c. The washing of the feet at the Last Supper.
d. Peter strikes off the ear of the High Priest's servant in the garden of Gethsemane.

RIGHT
e. Peter preaches to Cornelius' Gentile household when the Holy Spirit fills them (Acts 10:44).
f. Christ's Ascension.
g. Peter's release from prison.
h. Peter's crucifixion, upside down.

Incidentally this window is mostly painted, not stained, with the consequence that it may only rarely be washed, and even then most gently, or like the Cheshire cat it could fade away.

Most of the other windows in the church are filled with plain glass, which helps to ensure that the interior is generally well lit. The exceptions are the west window, largely obscured by the organ pipes, and the middle south-aisle window which is a memorial to the Matthews family dated 1874. You may love it or loathe it, but it is certainly a typical example of 1870s Victorian glass, strongly coloured and in perfect condition still. The stonework of each window in the aisles is of a different individual design and all are curiously wide for their height and utterly unmedieval.

The nave roof demands our attention, being an oak one of the highest quality. Prominent are the four carved and painted angels bearing shields. The north side pair carry the heraldic arms of Canterbury and the Diocese of Salisbury. The other two show St Peter's keys and the Tudor rose with the portcullis of France.

Fixtures and fittings are relatively few, although every memorial tells its story. By far the finest is in the south vestry, and therefore alas not accessible to casual visitors, although it may always be seen on request. It is a brass memorial plate dating from 1694 dedicated to Dorothy Williams. It represents her soul rising from the death bed with a scroll appropriately enough reading 'Death where is thy sting...'. Unusually Edmund Culpeper, the engraver, signed it.

On the wall of the south aisle is a fine First World War brass commemorating the deaths of Francis Old of the Dorset Yeomanry at Gallipoli in 1915 aged 21, and Captain Arthur McKenzie, MC, who died aged 28 in France in 1918. Intriguingly, directly underneath are two copper roundels, standard 1919 end-of-war issue, naming each man.

The list of rectors is displayed to the right of the organ; it only lacks the record of the earliest ones. As usual, some special people lie unobtrusively among them. There is, for example, Christopher Pitt, the subject of one of Dr Johnson's essays in his Lives of the Poets and definitely a minor poet, though well connected:

He was presented to the Rectory of Pimperne in Dorsetshire in 1722 by his relation Mr Pitt of Stratfield Saye in Hampshire [the estate given by a grateful nation to the Duke of

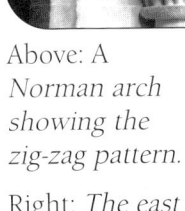

Above: *A Norman arch showing the zig-zag pattern.*

Right: *The east window, illustrating the life of St Peter in two sets of four panels set either side of the Crucifixion.*

Lest We Forget

THOSE WHO GAVE THEIR LIVES IN THE FIRST WORLD WAR LISTED ON THE MEMORIAL:

F.A.W. Old	A.M. McKenzie
W.J. Hunt	A.A. Hunt
H.J. Harding	E.W. Daniels
R.L. Richards	G.R. Barnett
H.N.T. Parmitter	A.H. Trim
G.J. Everett	E.J. Woodhouse

FURTHER INSCRIPTIONS IN THE CHURCH READ:

To the glory of God and in memory of Francis Old, 1st Dorset Yeomanry Missing in Gallipoli Aug. 21st 1915, Aged 21

Capt. Arthur McKenzie M.C. Royal Engineers who died and was buried in France Sept. 28th 1918 Aged 28. The gift of God is eternal life R.I.P.

Above: Dedication of the war memorial in 1919.

Left: The lychgate given by the Woodhouse family who lost three members during the two wars. Inscribed on the gate are the names of those who fell during the Second World War. Inscriptions on the lychgate read:

E. J. Woodhouse (Cambrai 1917) Lt. Col., Central India Horse; Oliver George Woodhouse (Dunkirk 1940). Major, Queens Own Royal West Kent Regt; Harold Sealy Woodhouse T.D. Colonel, Late Dorsetshire Regt. Blandford Camp 1943; Edgar Joseph Cutler, Royal Artillery, Somme 1940; Charles Geoffrey Richards, Wiltshire Regt. and Scottish Commandos, Syria 1941; William Albert Collier, R.N. Singapore 1942; Henry Lloyd Fletcher R.N. Alexandria 1943

Remembrance service with a detachment from HMS Collingwood, 1990s.

ST PETER'S CHURCH

The 14th-century preaching cross with post remaining from old pillory, c.1900.

Wellington after the battle of Waterloo]. His living was a place very pleasing by its situation and therefore likely to excite the imagination of a poet; where he passed the rest of his life, reverenced for his virtue and beloved for the softness of his temper and the easiness of his manners. Before strangers he had something of the scholar's timidity or distrust; but when he became familiar he was in a very high degree cheerful and entertaining. His general benevolence procured general respect; and he passed a life placid and honourable, neither too great for the kindness of the low, nor too low for the notice of the great.

Remarkable is that there were only three incumbents after Pitt's death in 1748 until 1862. George Bingham was rector until 1800 and is commemorated by two marble tablets in Latin on either side of the tower arch. His successor, Sir John Hanham, Bart., was a member of the Dean's Court family in Wimborne who had acquired that estate at the Dissolution of the Monasteries in 1547. Sir John, however, was over 80 when he accepted the Pimperne appointment and insisted that he should never be required to come here! His successor, Thomas Wyndham, took over in 1806 and was here until 1862 although never resident in the village. He did, however, for a short time in the 1840s, have Charles Kingsley of *The Water Babies* fame as his curate, by far the most eminent parson in the history of Pimperne's church.

The connections between Pimperne and Durweston were briefly very close since the Revd Lord Sydney Godolphon Osborne was Kingsley's brother-in-law. Sadly, Kingsley could not stand the contrast between the living standards of the gentry and the labourers hereabouts and when Eversley had a vacancy he moved and remained there for the rest of his life. His early death from pneumonia when he was only 56 was treated as a national disaster and such was his fame that his memorial is in Westminster Abbey.

Then there is James Hussey (1886–1906) who was the grandfather of Lord (Marmaduke) Hussey, the chairman of the BBC for a number of years in the 1980s and '90s.

Some assorted items in the church must not be overlooked. For instance, the main doors were installed in the old church in 1847 and their date in Roman numerals is marked on the inner side by domed studs. Next to the doors is a painted board (1846) giving details of the Ryves Charity provisions as laid down in 1685.

The chancel floor is generally covered by a large carpet made in 1926 by the Mothers' Union, helped by a few young men in the village. The Rector and Mrs Dittmer were responsible for its creation. The

Above left: Perpendicular tower with battlements added in the 1870s. In the foreground are the roots of the tree blown down in the great gale of January 1970. David Green was digging a grave at the time and only escaped by leaping into the grave as the tree came down!

Left: Another tree brought down in the churchyard.

Above: Extension to the burial ground behind the church, added in the 1970s.

splendid collection of kneelers was begun in the early 1970s to mark the centenary of the new church. It was Mrs Gladys Puckett's idea and Mrs Mary Burgess organised it. The kneelers were designed, worked and given by parishioners. Every rector since the rebuilding is commemorated by a kneeler, as are many Army regiments to which people in Pimperne belonged and other personal associations. Some speak of sermons in stone - there is also knowledge in needlework.

An Elizabethan chalice, assayed in Dorchester in 1556, is frequently used at Communion services. The church's records are complete since 1559 and are in the hands of the Dorset Archivist. They include a reference to a soldier from Cromwell's army who died in Pimperne on 16 January 1645. There is a special list of parishioners who died between 1706 and 1714 when 'all were buried in woollen (sic) according to ye Act of Parliament' - a requirement during those years to benefit the woollen industry and to spare the oak needed for ships fighting in the War of the Spanish Succession.

Also reported is the 18th-century fight between a gang of deer poachers headed by a Sergeant of Dragoons, who was a native of Pimperne surnamed Blandford, and the Keepers of Chettle Common. In the course of the affray Blandford's hand was cut off. Later 'it was buried in Pimperne churchyard with the honours of war!'

There are five bells in the tower, with framing sufficient for a sixth. One is inscribed William Pitt, George Selby, R.L. 1703. Another, recast in 1846, has its older inscription repeated in Lombardic lettering, 'Glory be to God on high.' The others are all dated 1891 having been given by the second Viscount Portman who inherited the title and estates in 1889.

There are a few points to be noted about the churchyard and its surroundings, an area enlarged in the 1970s by a gift of ground from the Coats family.

There is a fine stone war memorial commemorating the 12 Pimperne men who gave their lives in the First World War. The Woodhouse family lost three members in the two world wars, and gave the lych-gate in the late 1940s which lists all six men who died in the Second World War. Two gravestones were erected in the 1990s to commemorate men who died in May 1918 and (of wounds) in 1920: H.N.T. Parmiter (died 6 May 1918, aged 20) and G.J. Everett, (died 8 July, 1920, of wounds). Their families had not been able to afford headstones and the War Graves Commission were persuaded to provide them.

ST PETER'S CHURCH

Outside the gate is the 14th-century preaching cross erected for the use of friars, who were forbidden access to the church by the regular clergy. Its shaft was reduced in height in the 1650s by Cromwell's Act of Parliament against 'images'. This cross 'had had a crucifix at the top', and all crosses were to be cut down to 'the height of a man' - a tall one in this case! A groove cut into the base on its south side was once used to support a pillory.

What of the future? Everyone agrees that keeping the church in use is 'a good thing' - after all, a high proportion of the population wants it to be available for weddings, baptisms and funerals, let alone all those special occasions that relate to school functions, flower festivals, concerts, military commemorations and other communal activities. None of this, however, preserves the special place in people's affections that the church once had. Indeed, so long has it been the habit of relatively few people to go to church that there is more than a single generation who have never attended a service, even perhaps never entered such a building except out of curiosity. If you do not know the first thing about religion you cannot be expected to value the buildings which are its focal points.

So the danger for the future is of continuing widespread indifference. However, it should be a matter of some comfort that across the last 2000 years enthusiasm for the faith has ebbed and flowed. The appaling corruption of 16th-century Roman Catholicism led to the Reformation; the fanaticism of the 17th century was followed by the doubts of the 'enlightened' 18th century, only for that to give way to the astonishing enthusiasm of Victorian times, during which full tide Pimperne's church was rebuilt.

Since, therefore, there is the prospect of a revival of religious faith in the future, we must in our generation look after the building which will be of service to posterity, as well as ourselves using it regularly for the religious observances that are the primary reason for its existence. Further, let us not ignore the appeal of the church as an architectural treasure, as a container of works of art and design and as a record of social history that enriches the senses of any visitor.

Right: *Drawing of doorway and arch before their removal in 1874.*

PIMPERNE RECTORS

?–1299 Reginald de Cants
1299 Henry de la Hyde
1317 Nicholas de Legh
1348 Simon Clement
?–1379 John Losyn
1415 William Gray
? John Brockhill
1445 William Exatby
1447 Thomas Landover
1447 Tadmas Weldon
1509 Peter Rodinous
1520 Thomas Wever
1536 Christopher Morys
1547 John Elmer
1558 John Brock
1572 John Swaine
1619 Christopher Pitt
1642-1650 John White
1661 Christopher Pitt
1680 Henry Bailey
1682 John Home
1701 Thomas Stephens
1716 Henry Andrews
1722 Christopher Pitt
1748 George Bingham
1800 Sir John Hanham
1806 Thomas Wyndham
1862 William Bury
1886 James Hussey
1906 James Blunt Wilkinson
1911 Frank Bate
1915 Bathurst Wilkinson
1918 Ritchie Ashton Curtis
1923 Arthur Robert Dittmer
1936 Henry Noel Bridge
1937 Charles Louis Richards
1948 James Foxhall-Smedley
1968 Donald Farquharson-Roberts
1990 Gerald Squarey

Making horseshoes on the anvil outside the Forge. c.1910. Left to right: ?, ?, Reg Thorne.

A fallen tree outside the Forge. A branch had come off and killed the baker's horse. Jack Thorne is sitting on the tree, Reg and Frank James are standing in front.

Chapter 7
Pimperne People

with Roy Adam, Jack Thorne, Myrtle Churchill and Amy Hayter

While many villages are in decline, having lost their shop, school and pub, Pimperne is fortunate in that all of these facilities are not only active, but flourishing. This is due in no small measure to the development which has taken place and the way in which newcomers have integrated with locals to work together for the good of the community. None of the achievements of the past 40 years, the school swimming pool, the new Village Hall, sports ground and pavilion, would have been possible had a 'them and us' attitude prevailed.

The process was kick-started when 17 young families moved into new homes in Portman Road in 1961. They brought with them a variety of skills and backgrounds, but had all shared the uniting experience of the Second World War and perhaps it was this, combined with the common problems of struggling with mortgages and bringing up families that formed firm and lasting friendships. As one mum said 'We didn't have much money but we did have fun!' This was in the days before playschools, but the Portman Road children formed their own, with many enterprises from football and cricket on the island, camping in gardens, endless monopoly games and, in the summer, barbecues and beach parties at Studland.

There were memorable New Year parties (especially in 1963 when we floundered home through six feet of snow). Norman Pollard was a prime mover in the school swimming pool project, and the school's November Fayre, which still continues every year, was instigated with Doreen Kaile organising the well-remembered Monday evening sewing sessions (which often went on well into Tuesday morning!) producing aprons, tea cosies, etc. for the sales. Doreen came from Nottingham, but the Kaile family had lived in Pimperne for at least seven generations. St Peter's Close always enthusiastically supported these events, as did the whole village.

An informal walking group led by Jack Antell, Fred Waterman and Roy Biles explored (and got lost in) the surrounding countryside. For over 30 years these walks culminated in the New Year's Day walk to the Bugle Horn at Tarrant Gunville, when many a hangover was walked off! Sadly the Bugle closed a few years ago (*see page 6*).

Dorothy Kaile and John and Elizabeth Kaile at April Cottage, Anvil Road, 1922.

One of the more colourful characters in Portman Road was Colonel Bill O'Meara - an American colonel connected with Blandford Camp. He was a small man with a large labrador dog and a zippy two-seater MG sports car. The dog always sat up in the passenger seat beside Colonel Bill and, as the car was left-hand drive, the impression of a sports car being driven by a black labrador caused some near heart attacks for other motorists! Colonel Bill is also remembered for his party punch bowl - an innocuous tasting green mixture with pineapple floating in it, which caused one of his guests to see snakes crawling across the carpet in the small hours and left the rest with a three-day hangover! Perhaps it is just as well for the health of the village that Col Bill returned to California some years ago.

Happily each completed new development has brought its share of newcomers who have been welcomed into the village, who have entered enthusiastically into village life and made a valuable contribution to the community. The memories of some of the older residents of the village are recorded in the following pages.

Behind the bar at the Farquharson Arms, c.1980.
Left to right: Revd D. Farquharson-Roberts, Hazel Adam, Chaplain from the Camp, Roy Adam.
Note Roy's famous collection of whiskies on the top shelf.

Col Bill's farewell party, c.1980.
Left to right, back: Gordon Kaile, Brian Hunt, Fred Waterman, Trevor Wickham, Roy Adam, Roy Biles, Athol McCracken, Mervyn Williams, Jack Antell, Rick Ellis, Ken Edwards; middle: Beryl Kaile, Pat Hunt, Barbara Ellis, Betty Cochrane, Albert Cochrane, Hazel Adam, Joyce Wickham, Marjory Fuller, Nancy Williams, Bunty Antell, Mill Waterman, Anne Biles, Jean Coull, Doreen Edwards; front: Bob Fuller, Trevor, Dot, George Molony, May Molony, Bill O'Meara, Phyl House, Don House, Mary Moores, Peter Moores.

PIMPERNE PEOPLE

THE VILLAGE PUB
by Barbara Ellis

Cherished in the village as they grow fewer
Is that freemasonry of older stock,
Walking histories of times past.
They – who were the landlord of the pub,
Blacksmiths, maid, labourers and grooms –
Carry a frame of reference
Discrepant with present reality.
But prick them to reminiscence
And they map out their childhood space,
Rounded and bounded by the swelling downs,
Linked by chalky and unmetalled roads
To the distant unvisited towns.
This was their world, close and self-contained,
Inhabiting cottages long demolished,
Shaded by ancient elms, now felled or fallen,
The lanes all mired and trampled muck
Where cattle ambled to milking.
The brook flowed open then between green banks
Into a pond, scum speckled, freckled in spring
With frogspawn, its margins gilded with kingcups,
Where the great downland flocks, flowing
Like dirty foam down the long street, paused
For water on their way to market.
In those hard but halcyon remembered days
They came direct from school to milking shed
Or helped groom soft-breathed horses
Or picked up countless pails of stones for pence
In corded fields. They scrumped the russet apples
from the tree which still bears fruit at Five Ways
And as young lads and girls whispered and kissed
Pressed in the warm and yeasty darkness
Against the bakehouse wall.

And when in the long drawn winter evenings
The old men prattle in the public bar,
Newcomers listen attentively to their tales
Sharing vicariously this summoning of the past,
Till stumbling outside into the muffled night
Find themselves out of kilter with their time.
So telephone kiosk, ranks of waiting cars,
Even the new-built houses, neatly ranged,
All are drowned images only half perceived
Under the whispering wraithlike village.
Lying like water shimmering under the stars.

Coach outing from the Farquharson Arms to London, 1957.
Left to right, back: coach driver James, Alan Dennis, Alfie Wells, Arthur Upward, Ernie Vincent, Jack Sturmey, Ted Hayter, Roy Adam;
middle, standing: ?, S. Dellow, Mrs S. Dellow; middle seated: ?, ?, ?, Doug Simpson, John Shiner, Martin White, Jack Thorne, ? Brockway, ?, ?, Doug Simpson;
front: Joe Turner, Albert Wills, Jim Dean.

Roy Adam's mother with her brother and greyhounds behind the Farquharson Arms, 1906.

Roy Adam's mother and sister with one of the first cars in the village, c.1920.

PIMPERNE PEOPLE

Roy Adam

Roy Adam, Chairman of the Society of Dorset Men and a leading member of the Naval Association, was awarded the MBE in the Millennium Honours List. His family have lived in the village for five generations, his grandfather taking over the licence of the Farquharson Arms in the late 1800s and the pub remaining in the family until 1980. As well as being landlord, Joe Dowling was also a horse breaker and kept greyhounds and upwards of 40 horses. Roy has a wealth of Pimperne stories and here he recalls some of the characters and events of his youth:

When I was a boy in Pimperne there were many and various salesmen who journeyed for miles, some on foot, others by pony and trap or cart. One might say some of these salesmen were shabbily dressed and could have washed a little more often, but somehow I think they added a touch of colour to the rural scene.

I have a mental picture of a very small man calling on my mother on many occasions. Having displayed a variety of small articles such as cards of buttons, safety pins, reels of cotton and laces amongst other things, it was seldom he left without Mother making a purchase. He was referred to by some folks, more by way of identity than from an attitude of disrespect, as Mr Spotty Face. The facial blemish he was unfortunate to bear made its imprint on my youthful mind.

I remember particularly the man we called China Dickinson who lived near Blandford Railway Station with his horse and cart, who sold china, pots and pans and paraffin. The rattle and noise of his cart could be heard from a great distance especially on his journey home in the early evening, the tin pans hitting together. He wore a waistcoat with many buttons. As a sideline China Dickinson bought rabbit skins, paying two pence each, wild rabbits being the most common meal for country-dwellers as the countryside was heavily populated with rabbits. I used to enjoy fried rabbit, although it must be 30 years now since I have eaten one. Mr Dickinson covered a large area when on the Salisbury Road journey to Pimperne and the Tarrant Valley, Farnham, Minchington and in summertime to Handley and Woodyates.

I recall another salesman who lived in Pimperne; he used to sell bloaters and salt fish and he covered a large area like 'China', eventually owning a farm and numerous properties in the area. My father told me he was in the front line in Gallipoli at the tender age of 14 serving in the Royal Naval Division.

I call to mind a man with a black beard touched with grey who bore the nickname 'PegLeg'. He was usually accompanied by a lady, I think his wife, and their stock in trade consisted of clothes pegs, scrubbing brushes and small household requirements carried in a stout basket atop an old perambulator. This couple were familiar figures in most of the villages of North Dorset. I think they came from Shaftesbury and they were well received by most householders.

Another man called about once a year repairing umbrellas. He once carried out a repair for my mother and when she enquired how much, he replied 'Give me sixpence and a glass of beer Missus'.

Trooper Joe Dowling, of the Dorset Yeomanry, photographed c.1880 at Sturminster Newton.

We used to see many more gypsies than we do today. I remember women who would reluctantly buy sprigs of heather or clothes pegs rather than incur the displeasure or anger of the caller. It was surprising the number of people who were scared of gypsies because of the belief that if offended the gypsy would lay some terrible curse on you. Those parting words of a gypsy after having made a sale 'God bless you, me dear, you'll never want' brought feelings of relief to many an ill-at-ease housewife.

I write only of Pimperne, where I have lived all my life; it is very rare one gets gypsy callers these days. Indeed I know of cases where gypsies have forsaken the wandering life for a more static existence, often working on the land and proving themselves hardworking and law-abiding members of society.

In early December two elderly and most pleasant nuns, possibly from Wimborne, called each year. Mother always gave them a donation and sometimes a cup of tea or coffee, afterwards signing their little book recording the amount given. Another well-known visitor year after year

Mary Ann Bull, known as the 'Reddle Woman', with her cart outside the Union Arms, Acreman Street, Cerne Abbas, c.1900. She is being greeted by the landlord of the pub, Charlie Fox. She died at the age of eighty in 1917. (See also The Book of Cerne Abbas.*)*

was Mary Ann the Reddle Woman with her brown pony and bright red four-wheeled open van; to the children of the neighbourhood she was wrapped in mystery, a witch-like being who brewed charms and magic potions in a little black pot on the fire of sticks beside her tent. Her name was Mary Ann Bull and she hailed from Somerset. The reddle was obtained from Cornwall and at sheep-dipping time she would peddle her wares, also selling brickdust for cleaning harness.

According to my late mother, Mary Ann had a weather-beaten countenance and wore layers of petticoats, which made a good hiding place for her monies. Apparently she used to trust her monies to various publicans and collect it on the journey home. She frequently made use of my grandfather, Joe Dowling, who was a horse dealer and held the licence of the Farquharson Arms in the late 1800s until 1917. Mary Ann smoked a pipe and was possessed of a very bad temper, similar to the lurcher dog that was tied to her cart. As with true Romanies today she knew the value of many herbs and would prescribe cures for many ailments.

My grandfather always purchased a good number of horses at Shroton Fair and Woodbury Hill Fair near Bere Regis. Mary Ann was a regular. She slept under bags and canvas beneath the cart, guarded by her faithful dog. I well remember the late PC, Charles Northover, telling me of being called to where Mary Bull was very ill under the cart. Before anything could be done the dog had to be destroyed. Somehow, I think this was in Stourpaine chalk pit, now the site of a splendid residence. However, the lady was removed to Cerne Abbas Union, and now rests in Sydling Churchyard near Dorchester, being laid to rest in the heart of the county which had made this outstanding character so welcome, as much for the wares she peddled as for herself.

PIMPERNE PEOPLE

JACK THORNE

Jack Thorne was born in 1903 in the house by the Old Forge next to what is now the Anvil Hotel. Like his father before him, he was the village blacksmith and lived and worked there until his retirement in the 1970s, when he moved to a bungalow in Frampton Road. In an interview in 1990 he told of the changes that had taken place in the village over the previous 80 years:

I went to the village school when it was new-built [the present school opened in 1908]. There were three classes, Mr Fry was our schoolmaster and took the seniors, Mrs Fry had the juniors and Miss Sly, she had the infants when I first went to school. We had a gravel playground, we used to play football and we were always getting in the wrong for breaking the windows! They were very strict at school. I was a bit of a nuisance, so they put me amongst the girls for copying, but it didn't make a lot of difference! 'Course we only had half our schooling; if my father said 'I want you today' we just stayed home – there weren't the restrictions there are today.

I learnt baking as a boy at the old bakery (opposite the Farquharson Arms). Mrs Jeffery owned the bakery and shop – her husband's horse ran away with him and killed him. They had four men working in the bakery besides another woman in the shop as well as Mrs Jefferies. In those days we used to deliver groceries all around Pimperne, part of Blandford, Langbourne, Langton, across the downs to Hinton and Chettle, Gunville, Launceston and Monkton. We used to go every other day taking groceries, bread and cakes. On Mondays she used to say to me 'Hitch the horse in the cart Jack.' I would only be nine or ten years old. 'Go up to Foxwarren, Lord Portman's keeper's cottage, and then go on up to three families at Newfields Farm.'

You know what families were in those days – they had not 2lb loaves, but 4lb and groceries too if they had ordered them – I used to do that three times a week. Going through Newfield Bottom in winter I have known the water up to the pony's belly – the water used to come up through Pimperne just the same. 'Course Taylor used to put the hatch in the other side of the bridge, used to divide the water to his meadows for the dairy cows, he used to keep a man for three months special to put the water off here or there 'cause they had hatches in all the fields round there. All these farmers did in those days, it was to get early feed for the cows, but you don't get that now.

When we were boys the soldiers used to come down from the camp in the First World War, used to bet each other they couldn't jump over the stream – lots of them fell in! My father once saved a girl from drowning; she fell in and he jumped in and fished her out. I tell people they never know what village life was like in those days 'cause you had the open downs, you could walk up there on to the open downs in those days, all rabbits and larks – you never hear larks now.

I learnt the trade from my father. I mind the first horse I shoed, there was this quiet horse, father said 'Go on and shoe it!' He always said he could tell by ear whether that nail were right or wrong. 'Course that's the big thing in shoeing horses, knowing where you are putting the nails. With racehorses you got very little to play with, your shoes got to fit, if you get inside you are into blood. I can put on that hand when I went wrong. I could always tell, people never realise with shoeing horses what a job it is. My father used to get up about half-past six and keep shouting up the stairs 'You getting up?' We used to start work at seven, always go shoe-making and then go back to breakfast and go on from there, we never stopped any more after that.

A summer job was putting bonds [rims] on wagon wheels – we used to have four men on that. The rims would get loose and if they weren't done the wheel would fall to pieces. What we had to do was cut a piece out of them, shut them up again making them about three-quarters of an inch smaller than the wheel, then put them in the pit and put faggots on them to warm them up. We used to light the fire at half-past three in the morning, by six o'clock we had them all on the wheels – the carts were off down to the brewery and we were sat down having some beer! I'd as soon have a cup of tea!

I left school when I was 13 and went to Letton House in the stables; I got 12 shillings a week, that were a seven-day week; well, we had to go in on Sunday mornings – no holidays. What I really wanted to do was go in the Army. The recruiting

THE BOOK OF PIMPERNE

Jack Thorne at the door of the Forge, c.1930.

The Forge in the snow, 1963.

Jack Thorne shoeing a horse, c.1930.

Fitting metal rims to wooden cartwheels, 1920s.

Fun Football, in celebration of Queen Elizabeth's accession, 1953, in Old Football Field. Left to right, back: B. Miles, E. Barnett, R. Dacombe, E. Miles, C. Coats, J. Thorne, A. Wells; front: T. Henderson, J. Sturmey, M. White, A. Upward, E. Joyce, G. Elliott.

Jeffery's bakery and horse and trap, c.1910.

officer was always after me, so I joined the Queens Own Dorset Yeomanry; I did five years. I joined as a blacksmith [rather than as a farrier]; they had just done away with horses. The CO wanted me to go on a course as a gun fitter, but my father got ill just about that time, so that was finished.

I never knew what holidays were really. You might get a day off or a couple of days when you wanted it, but in my job, 'specially after my father died and I was left on my own, I never had nobody there.

Do you know I had over 100 carthorses in this village? I had 30 on Manor Farm and then there were eights and tens all round, over 100 horses besides all the other things - we had all the implements to repair in those days. The worst time was in the thirties when there was a big slump in farming. All the farmers grassed down their farms so that meant there was very little used of anything - they could buy grain for about five bob a hundredweight - imported that was, when the slump was on - but it got better.

When the Second World War came along things were different altogether. You were wanted more. 'Course in the First World War we were blacksmiths for MacAlpine, building the Camp. We cut all the rails and that when they put the railway in. Sir Lindsey Parkinson did the building at the camp. In the second war we were blacksmiths again and they sent me down a lad, blacksmith's mate, who was paid by the Camp.

With the metal work I had lads helping me in the back end. They came on a five-year apprenticeship - every year their wages would go up. 'Course in my day there wasn't the money about there is in the present day. When I finished work I was only getting two guineas a set for shoeing, 'course there was extra for studs, etc. Nowadays for a big hunting horse it's anything £14, £15, £16 and, if you have to go there, another fiver. [In 2000 this is more like £35-45 plus a visit charge.]. Long before the First World War Fred Walters used to rent the farm and he planted the chestnut trees by the church. His father and brother had Studhouse as a racing stable, they used to go up the track to the Camp, there was a mile and a half gallop up there and they used to have a brick-built rubbing-down house for the horses up there too.

I looked after a racing stable at Stourpaine before the last war. They had over 20 horses, I was over there five mornings a week and then sometimes at four o'clock in the afternoon. You wasn't allowed in the stables before four o'clock 'cause it was rest time for the horses. The lads went to dinner at one o'clock and they didn't get back 'till four to do the horses up; that was their rest time too.

Then we used to have to work on till six or seven o'clock. There was a lot of work in the racing stable. Some days I had to put on over 30 plates of a morning, specially when Sandown were on 'cause they had a military meeting at Sandown, the officers, they had their horses - you had all the plates to put on and the day after tomorrow you had to be there to take the plates off and put on the ordinary shoes again. [Horses wear thin aluminium shoes for racing and farriers change the shoes before and after a race.].

I was Chairman of the Parish Council and Chairman of the Parish Hall Committee. I was Captain of the Bellringers. We have done a lot of ringing. There is no village around here that has had more ringing than this village has. We used to ring Sunday morning and Sunday evening every week and we had seven or eight bellringers. We were going to have the bells hung up one time and I spent one or two afternoons up there with people coming to look at them from Loughborough and you know what? They offered to re-hang and re-tune they bells for £600 and you would not get that done for £12 000 today!... We said these bells are in such a state we won't ring them any more. 'Course Stourpaine came over and rung them occasionally - hop and jump about after you have rung them!

I learnt bellringing in the church when I was 16 and sang in the choir when I was 9. When we were boys we had Sunday School in the hall and we had to march from there to church on Sunday mornings. We had Sunday School outings, used to go sometimes to Badbury Rings in the old horse and brakes; sometimes we used to go off by train from Blandford Station.

Those were the days with the cricket team; old Tom Barnett, my father, the racehorse trainers and the farmers all played cricket for Pimperne. It was a different atmosphere, used to go from one village to another in the old horse and brake.

Pimperne is nothing like a village now, we had everything going on in those days, fancy-dress fêtes, a football team, a lovely billiards table in the Men's Club, flower shows, there was all sorts going on. When you come to look back on it the atmosphere was different altogether.

THE BOOK OF PIMPERNE

Deans Court, Wimborne, built 1725 around the medieval Deanery of Wimborne.

Myrtle, the maid in the white collar, watching from the window the presentation from the inhabitants of Wimborne, tenantry and friends in the neighbourhood to Sir John Hanham Bt., on his coming of age in 1919.
Left to right on the steps: Lady Hanham, Maud Hanham, ?, Sir John Hanham, ?.

PIMPERNE PEOPLE

Myrtle Churchill

At the time of the interview in 1995 Myrtle was approaching her 90th birthday and nearly blind, but her enthusiasm for cooking and gardening was undiminished, although she complained that her family had taken her electric hedge trimmer away (after she had twice cut through the cable!). Married to Jack, a gamekeeper, Myrtle had a great capacity for enjoying life and was greatly loved by her large family of children and grandchildren. Here she describes days in service before her marriage.

I left school at 14 and went to work at Brog Farm, Corfe Mullen. I used to help to do the washing on Mondays; you had a bowl on the table washing the socks, I couldn't reach and I had to kneel on a chair to reach the bowl! They were quite strict - if they said you had to be in, you had to be in. I lived in although I could walk home in a quarter of an hour. I went into one of the farm labourer's cottages one day 'cause there were boys and girls my age and I got told off considerably! They thought I was going to talk about what went on in the farm!

From there I went to Deans Court in Wimborne for Lady Hanham as a between maid. You had to work in the morning till twelve o'clock in the house and then in the kitchen. There was Lady Hanham and her two sons and a daughter - Sir John had died before I went there. She never had the room where he used to sit opened again - I never seen in there all the time I was there. When they all died, they had nobody to leave it to and the place went to a cousin. The gardens were opened and I went to have a look round and I said I used to be there and she showed me all over the house and that was the first time I saw in that room; I used to always wonder about it.

There was a butler, a cook, a housemaid and the gardener's daughter, who used to come in daily. There was ever such wide steps, I scrubbed them all one day and she gave me five shillings - that was a lot then. I had about £20 a year.

I had my own room there, I had a little room and you had to go through my room to get to the cook's room. I used to read when I went to bed and, of course, it was candles in those days. Lady Hanham used to have a storeroom opposite my bedroom and she used to come up often to get things out at night - I was supposed to be asleep so when I heard her coming I took the candle in bed, held the bedclothes up, went on reading and I must have gone to sleep. The bedclothes came down and of course I had a burnt bed! I felt meself burning that's what woke me up and the smoke woke the cook up!

I got up next morning and went down and lit the kitchen range. All I wanted to do was see someone and tell 'em what I'd done, I had to get it off my chest! Anyway Miss Hanham came down to let the cats in and I told her straight away. Nobody else was up, I told her what I'd done - I burnt my hair as well as the bed. I had long hair then, wore it done up in a bun on top, and d'you know, they never said a cross word to me, they were ever so nice - told me not to have a candle in bed again! Well I didn't do that again!

Myrtle Churchill as a young girl.

I got up about six or six-thirty and I had to light the fires; there was a big hall - about 20 foot - had all polished floor, and I used to have to polish that with beeswax and turpentine. You scraped your beeswax off and put the turpentine with it and rubbed it in the floor and then you had a cloth and polished it, and you used to be able to see your face in that floor - it was lovely! But it was hard work really, and they had a big fireplace where you put big logs - it was a lovely room. There were two big drawing rooms and a dining room, of course, there wasn't even Hoovers them days. We used to sprinkle damp tea leaves and brush the carpet - not fitted carpets, they had fringes round - you brushed the carpet every day with this big broom, 'course you can imagine all the dusting that had to be done with all this dust flying around.

She used to send for cakes to London, to the Corner House, beautiful cakes they were, all on the side in the dining room - she used to give me a bit occasionally! I can see that tea service and dinner service now. It was a lovely service with a blue line round it and gold trimming and then little roses, of course it was soda to wash up with them days but you used to have to wash it with clear water, no soda because it would bring the pattern off, it was lovely and they were so particular.

They had a big dog everybody used to be frightened of, a St Bernard, and I used to have to go out with Miss Hanham to do her animals. I had to learn to milk the cows - I was milking cows in amongst everything else!

Keepers at Turnworth, c.1920s Jack Churchill is on the right.

PIMPERNE PEOPLE

We didn't get much time off; one Sunday we had the afternoon and evening off and had to be in at 9 or 10 o'clock, the next Sunday we didn't have any time off at all. We had a half day in the week - you imagine people today - well they wouldn't do it. Then there wasn't much chance to do anything else - you left school and you were packed off into service.

I was there four years. Lady Hanham said, when I left, I had to go out and buy something to remember my time at Deans Court. And I'd seen a brooch that I liked, I had looked at it in the shop many times, and I bought it; it cost £4 - that was a lot of money then - and she give me the money for it to remember the time I had there. I got letters and photos that Lady Hanham wrote to me up until I was married.

I left there and went to Turnworth. I worked for the Parry-Ogdens who were related to the Hambros; the lady was a Hambro before she was married, and she had a big family of children and she used to carry on with all the men on the farm that she could! She was always out waiting for them! I went there as kitchen maid and I got on ever so well with the cook and I was there four years.

I met Jack at Turnworth when he was still in the Navy - Jack's father was keeper and the cook was going to marry his brother. Jack had joined the Navy when he was 18 and when I went to Turnworth he was in India but they had it all planned that I should meet him. The cook was ever so fond of Jack, she had known him from a little boy, it's funny how things work out isn't it? I told you how the lady used to be very friendly with all these farm hands - Jack was the only boy that was allowed in the house that I know of! When he was home on leave and I was on duty he used to come down in the kitchen all afternoon and evening.

I had to cook a lunch and dinner every day. I had to get up, light the kitchen range, lay out the kitchen table for the cook and if anything wasn't quite clean I nearly got it thrown at me but I got on ever so well with that cook. It was all copper pans and we used to have to clean them with salt and vinegar. You had them out in the sink and rubbed all the backs with salt and vinegar mixed together and then washed them out with cold water and then you had to get them really dry, otherwise there would be dark marks all over them; they weren't cleaned with brasso or anything, but every so often they would have them re-tinned inside.

I had to prepare the game and I used to hate doing it; it would be all crawling with maggots, but the cook did say 'you make these cakes for me' and she would do it. She would get them on the table and draw their innards out and the maggots would be all crawling up her arms - she didn't mind a bit! But they had to be like that before they thought they were fit to be eaten, everything had to be hung and they never had any fridge or freezer. They had a big larder and half a lamb used to come and different meats - all hung up in this larder and you cut a shoulder off or cutlets when you wanted it. Cutlets were cut to the bone and little paper frills put on the bone - they bought the little paper frills.

Anne Dennis and Myrtle Churchill enjoying an ice cream on a Lunch Club outing to West Bay, c.1990.

We made our own baking powder and ground our own pepper and coffee. You had to grind the coffee in the morning and if I ground it at night Mrs Ogden would come out and tell me off - it had to be fresh - she knew I'd done it! In the mornings before you could boil a kettle you had to get the stove nearly red hot because you had to make scones for breakfast and you had to call the cook with hot water and a cup of tea.

They never expected to see the servants when they came down to breakfast so you had to be finished downstairs and then go upstairs and make the beds and do the bedrooms - they didn't want to see servants - and then we had to be finished to go for prayers in the dining room in Turnworth House. All the staff had to sit behind the screen and Colonel Ogden's brother, William, used to take the service every morning so we had to get our work done first - I don't really remember, but I suppose he read the Bible or something and said prayers.

Mrs Parry Ogden was deaf and she used to always play the organ in church; we all had to sit in the choir whether we could sing or whether we couldn't and half way through the service when she used to sing funny and if we weren't singing she used to shout 'Sing Up Sing Up!' We used to have to go to church every Sunday morning, so *when we had our afternoon off we didn't get out until about four o'clock.*

Every day the floors had to be cleaned. We used to clean the vegetables and get everything ready for Sunday on Saturday and we always used to have roast beef in the summer and boiled beef in the winter on Sundays with all the vegetables and a fruit pudding like a Christmas pudding. They had a special one for the dining room and these had to be done Saturday - Canns plum pudding - it was lovely really, there was only a quarter pound of raisins that was the only fruit that was in it, and a lot of suet, more suet than flour - but it was lovely. They used to have that every Sunday right through the winter till Easter. Easter Sunday we had a tart. That went on all summer, always had the same; it's funny - they wouldn't think of doing that now.

We used to have hares and rabbits; we had to sit them up on the dish, not break them at all and you had to skin them and leave the ears on, put them in boiling water and scrape the hairs off them then you had to put them sitting up on the dish, skewered, so they looked just as if they were ready to run. It used to look nice. The butler used to carve it. It used to be sent up on a lift and put on the trolley and sent along to the dining room.

I was supposed to cook the staff's dinner; we had the same sort of things as they had in the dining room but not so fancy. The pudding we had on Sunday, I suppose a lot of people would have thought was better than they had in the dining room with their Canns plum pudding. All of the kitchen staff used to sit down together in the kitchen, the scullery boy, two housemaids, butler and parlourmaid.

When I went to Turnworth Mr and Mrs Parry Ogden were both invalids and there was a night nurse and a day nurse - she had stopped rushing around then! I was there four years and then I went to Corfe Mullen, opposite the church, as cook - my sister was parlourmaid and my father was gardener. My father, Harry Lucas, was a baker by rights, but he had a bad heart and he couldn't stand the heat.

After I had been at Corfe Mullen two years Jack had been invalided out of the Navy after five years and was keepering. We got married and went to Uddens near Wimborne to live. It was nice up there and I'm still friendly with a woman up there now.

Top: *The four Churchill brothers in 1918, Jack, Tom, Harry and Cecil.*

Right: *Myrtle Churchill with daughter Barbara in 1935.*

PIMPERNE PEOPLE

AMY HAYTER

A former President of Pimperne WI, Mrs Amy Hayter played a valued part in all village activities for over 30 years, as did her husband Ted. She was famous in the village for her cooking and handicrafts. Here she tells of her early days in service in the big house of a nearby village in the 1920s:

I was 14 in 1926 when I started work as a kitchen maid in a children's hospital in Swanage. I had to be up about half-past six to get the fire going in the kitchen. The food was quite good, the cook was Matron's sister, she was slightly deaf but she always heard what you didn't want her to hear! My father had died when I was seven and this cook kept on at me, so after a few months my mother came and took me home. She thought it would be nice for me to be in a big house with more girls, so I went as between maid at Iwerne House (now Clayesmore School).

I started work at half-past six in the housekeeper's room. There was the grate to lay and then I went into the still room to wash up the breakfast things. There was another between maid, Margaret, and we had to do the footmen's bedrooms and their washbasins and things like that, and the valet - we used to have terrific fun with him - he didn't know we laughed at him! As it is in all big houses, he had a crush on the cook. At lunch time he came up into the larder and they always had a case of ale and they would have their elevenses there, drinking this glass of beer. Oft times they would fall out. Everyone knew that he was a very good pianist and he used to play this particular tune, 'I will take her back if she wants to come back' and I would think 'Oh they have made it up again!'

I used to go out in to the scullery part of the kitchen to do all of the vegetables; there were four big wooden sinks and we used to wash up in one, put clear water in the next to rinse it, then there was another one where we used to do the vegetables. There was a whopping great table in the middle and flagstones on the floor. The kitchens were in the basement and there was a path outside where you could walk around the house. I had to keep the scullery clean - not the kitchen, we had two kitchen maids to do that and a scullery maid. After a time they asked me if I would like to be scullery maid and I liked that better. I liked cooking and I could watch how it was done but I didn't like housework at all!

The housekeeper was in charge. I think I must have been very fortunate really; in no job I went to was I really unhappy. If it was a lady we didn't like then we didn't stay, but mostly it was the other

Amy Hayter (right) with Margaret, c.1930.

staff that caused trouble I found, not the people of the house. In the big house we hardly saw them at all. Once I was going across the passage with the housekeeper's afternoon tea and Mr Ismay came down the passage to use the phone. It meant I should go right back down the passage into the still room and put the tray down to open the door for him, but he said 'Come along' and opened the door for me - I was just a young girl and I thought 'Fancy a gentleman opening a door for me!'

The Ismays were very nice to the village - if the young ladies went down to the school and saw a child without a pair of shoes they were down there with a pair. They used to treat the villagers very kindly, very fair I think. We had a dance once a fortnight in the Village Hall - that was a hall the Ismays had put up for the village - and film shows, sixpence and a shilling; if we felt a bit better off we would go in the shilling seats! We used to have some lovely times there.

The Ismays had three daughters, it was a second marriage and he had two daughters by his first wife, one of them was married and lived at Hanford House. There were over 20 of us in the house - butler, three footmen, hallboy, odd-job

THE FLETCHERS

Clockwise from top: *Harry and Louisa Fletcher, c.1917; Myrtle Fletcher in Land Army uniform, 1943; Myrtle entering the church on the arm of her father, Harry Fletcher; Ted Barnett (Sgt. Dorset Regt.), Myrtle, Audrey Fletcher, ?, Nina White, Pimperne Church 1946; Lloyd Fletcher, November 1940 (killed in action 1943).*

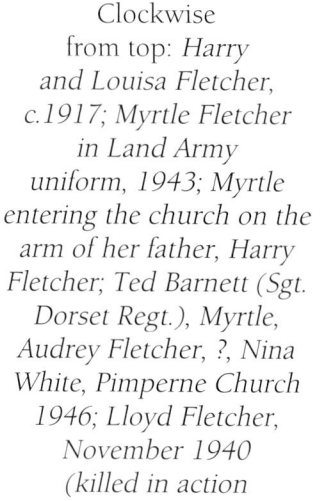

Ted Hayter, a much-loved character in Pimperne, drawing raffle tickets, old Village Hall, 1988.

man, housekeeper, cook, three kitchen maids, scullery maid, two between maids, three housemaids and head housemaid, two lady's maids, nanny and governess for the young ladies.

Outside they had two kitchen gardeners, father and son, and the other gardeners used to come and do the flowers. I used to have to put the knives out every morning for the hallboy to clean. One day he was very busy, there was a party and he had all the knives from the butler's office upstairs to clean and he told me he wouldn't have time to do the kitchen knives. I said 'I'm sorry, it's my job to leave them, you must do as you like.' I got half way back up the passage and there was a clatter, clatter – he was throwing the jolly lot of the kitchen knives at me! The butler came out of his office and wanted to know what was going on, but they weren't terribly strict in that house, it was really happy there, we all mucked in. The butler used to laugh with us if we had a joke, but the housekeeper thought it was a little bit much and we would have to stop, but the butler didn't mind his boys talking to us.

I used to get seven shillings and sixpence a week, £3 a month. We didn't get holidays as such; after we had been very busy in the winter with parties and shoots and that, we used to have a day off.

My uncle had worked on building the Pavilion at Bournemouth and we said we would go in to the opening, so on our bikes and away we went. We left our bikes at Poole and took the bus into Bournemouth. We waited about an hour for the Duke of Gloucester to come, then someone said he had already been! Anyway, we made good use of the rest of the day and had a good day out in Bournemouth.

We had to provide our own uniforms; three white aprons and two print dresses for mornings and black dresses for the afternoon. There was never no central heating, you had to take water up in a big brass can, turn the beds down and stand the can filled with hot water in the basin and put a cosy over it to keep it hot. They had a huge cupboard where they used to dry the hunting kit. They had their own laundry with three laundry maids by the stables and the bothy where the grooms who didn't live in the village slept.

The butler wasn't above playing jokes. One time he rang Home Farm and told them Lord Stalbridge was coming to see over the farm and would they see it was well tidied up. When the milk boy came down in the afternoon 'Gosh' he said 'You'd never believe what's been going on up farm today – the dairy and the bacon factory and all the farm have been all done up!' Then the butler said 'Don't they know its April 1st!'

They made all their own butter in the dairy at Home Farm and many a time I came down to the house with a side of bacon or a whole lamb on my handlebars. They used to have grouse and partridges from Scotland and venison and snipe – they didn't draw them at all. The staff all had very good food as well as the family, 'specially the kitchen staff.

I stayed about three years at Iwerne House and later I worked in a Rectory. I found people like rectors were much different to people like the Ismays in the way they regarded you – at least the rectors' wives seemed to look down on you more. In the Rectory we never got turkey for Christmas Day; they had it and we had to have rabbit pie.

It was all lamps and candles and stone hot-water bottles in those days, but we used to make our own fun, we always made the best of things.

THE BOOK OF PIMPERNE

Early Days - Mrs Rushbridge with the Playschool in the old Village Hall, 1969.

Youth Club party in the old Village Hall, 1952, to celebrate the first leave of three sailors who had joined the Navy at the same time. Left to right, back: K. Taylor, Billy Witt, Vic Miles, Fred Vane, Peter Cann, Richard Brooks, Peter Mullins, Len Vincent, Derek Rayment, Reg. Joyce; 3rd row: Tony Mundy, Desmond Tuckett, Pauline Whitely, Tony Dacombe, Mike Dennis, David Langdown, Audrey Mullins, Derek Waygood, Philip Collier; 2nd row: Thelma Pope, Judy Tunstall, Christine Hobson, Mrs Whitely (leader), Pearl Fripp, Stella Langdown, Barbara Fripp; front: ? Brooks, Tony Ellis, Margaret Collier, John Langdown, Percy Osment.

Chapter 8
Groups, Shows and Celebrations

with contributions from Connie Johnston and Roy Adam

WOMEN'S INSTITUTE, ART AND DRAMA

In the early part of the 20th century, when the lives of countrywomen were often restricted to home and village, the Women's Institute provided opportunities to learn new skills, make new friends further afield and have a voice in national affairs. For more than 50 years Pimperne WI played a leading role in village life. Connie Johnston, former WI Secretary, looks back on their achievements:

Pimperne WI was formed in February 1944 and soon a thread of friendship was spun to include nearby villages, which formed our local group. We then joined in with activities within the county of Dorset and participated within the National Federation of Women's Institutes. For country housewives who had long been isolated in their village communities it really was a window of opportunity on the world and it was not long before Pimperne WI formed overseas links starting with an Institute in Tasmania and ending, 50 years later, with a link in the USA.

It soon became clear that the monthly WI meetings were generating many ideas which were of benefit to the village and places further afield. A Christmas party was arranged each year for the village children and, as the years passed, annual outings for the housebound. Bazaars, fêtes, flower shows and sporting events could always count on the WI to man stalls, make tea and bake an unending stream of mouth-watering cakes and savouries.

In 1944 a dance was organised which proved so successful that a donation of £77.6s.10d. was sent to the British United Aid to China charity (a lot of money at this time when a farmworker's basic wage was about £6 a week). This

Above: *Mrs Ayres (left) in the outfit she wore to Buckingham Palace, with Mrs Alner, 1965.*
Below: *Garden Meeting, Little Treddington, 1962. Left to right, back: Mesdames Hayter, Tinsley, Rogers, Ellis, Garnsworthy, Phillips, Tucker, ?, Hunt, Langdown, Banks, Molony, Hewitt, Daniels, Holland; front: Miles, Alner, Ridout, Rayment, ?, White, Reed.*

*Baby Show, 1947, judged by Dr G. Forge and Nurse Hawkins.
Left to right, back: Doris Banks, Vera Brett, Mrs Harding, Rene Avery, Win Sturmey, Mrs Trickett, ?, ?, Mrs Ridout; front: Alice Langdown, ?, Mrs Henderson, Mrs North, ?, Joan Bailey and her mother each holding a twin, ?.*

GROUPS, SHOWS AND CELEBRATIONS

WI members in the 1940s. Left to right, facing camera: Mesdames D. Banks, Fletcher, E. Pike, M. Barnett, Wray-Cooke, B. Miles, P. North, D. Rayment.

Pancake Race, 1993. Left to right: Sue Hatchard, Janet Parker, Barbara Ellis, Anne Allan, Win Usher.

Jack and the Beanstalk, *1990*.
The picture includes: *Millie Waterman, Barbara Ellis, Connie Johnston, Kay Knight, Doreen Hewlett, Irene Dowdeswell, Audrey Daniels, Grace Abbey, Jean Coull, Muriel Reed.*

Puss in Boots, *1988*.
The picture includes: *Betty Ryland, Audrey Daniels, Grace Abbey, Doreen Hewlett, Jean Coull, Millie Waterman, Jack Whale, Phyl Rabbitts, Eileen Lancaster, Muriel Reed, Barbara Ellis, Kay Knight, Doris Hinton, Joan Bateman, Joyce ?.*

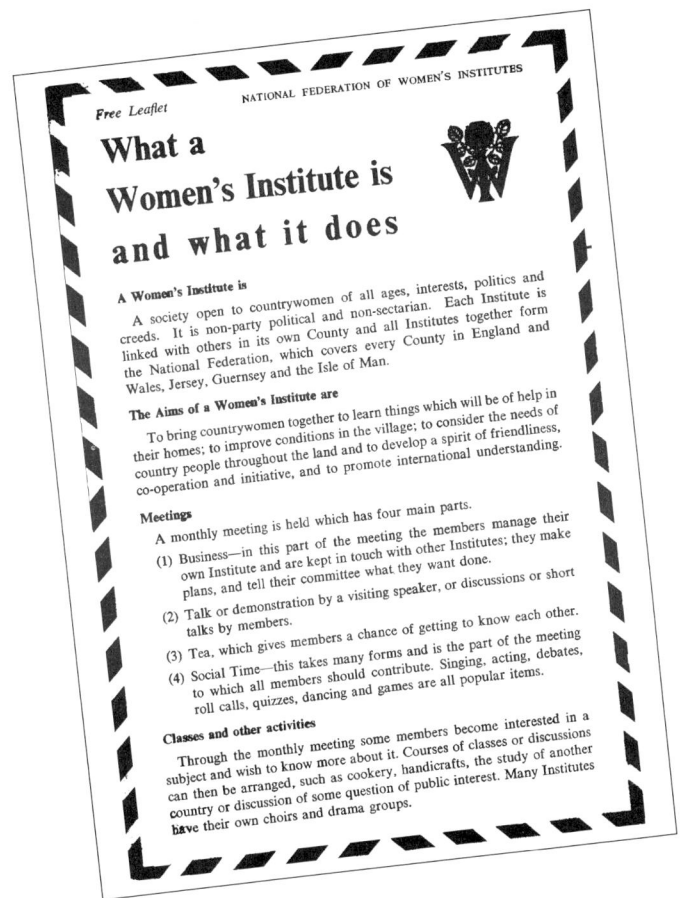

Left: 'What a WI is' leaflet, 1962.
Above: Miss Richardson presenting the Jubilee Cake at the WI Garden Meeting, July 1965.

was followed in 1945 with an event to raise funds for the 'Help Holland Council'. Generosity to worthy causes continued through the years; St Dunstans, Sue Ryder, Lifeboats and many more brought our donations into the 1990s.

Our Institute was also full of fun. Each month a speaker was invited who amused, entertained and often educated an avid audience. One talk was entitled 'Mad Passionate Love' and the 1950s audience's reaction was not recorded when the talk proved to be about a deep love of the Dorset countryside! It was also surprising, when a speaker failed to appear, just how talented the WI members were. Songs, poems, or an anecdote or two soon made a spoilt afternoon into a palace of varieties.

Pimperne WI was reported in a number of publications. Home and Country reported a debate on 'What would improve my cottage' and Pimperne's suggestion was 'Better sanitation and a bathroom'. How things have changed! In 1945, at the Annual Conference in Dorchester, a motion was put forward regarding second postal deliveries in villages. Pimperne reported that the Rural Council had built a new estate (St Peter's Close) but the postman only delivered to the corner of the Close on his second delivery. The Postmaster in Blandford had refused to increase the delivery area as the expense would not be justified. Our speaker declared 'as the postman comes on his bike and it would only take him five minutes, I fail to see where the expense comes in.' And here we are in the year 2000 with only one delivery!

At the 1945 AGM in London a resolution was put forward by Pimperne 'that more homes for old people should be provided and that husbands and wives should be able to stay together and not be parted.' This resolution shows that the old workhouse conditions were quite a recent memory and is a reminder of how much progress has been made since the war.

The Flower Show was a much enjoyed annual event organised by the WI. In 1945 it was held in the garden of Hyde Farm by permission of Mr and Mrs Charles Coats. There were side-shows, dancing by the school's junior pupils and the WI Folk Dancing Class. The proceeds went to the village 'Welcome Home Fund' for servicemen returning from the war. From 1975 the Flower Show was organised jointly by the WI and Garden Club with a committee headed by Betty Ryland, Doris Hinton and Jean Coull.

Another much loved part of village life was the Pimperne Drama Group. This started with a Christmas show produced by Mrs Phyl House but in later years became a series of memorable annual pantomimes written, directed and produced by Jack Whales, who also wrote the words and music to the very catchy and topical songs. One of the most outstanding was Jack and the Beanstalk.

THE BOOK OF PIMPERNE

Top: *Making a wall hanging, 1992.*
Left to right: Doris Duncan, Maureen Moss, Lorna Stewart, Mary Moores,
Connie Johnston, Barbara Ellis, Muriel Reed.
Above: *The finished article.*

GROUPS, SHOWS AND CELEBRATIONS

Who will forget Jack and his mother worried about payment of the Poll Tax? The cow costume was made by Doris Duncan and filled by Irene Dowdeswell and Doris Hinton - a cow much addicted to boogie dancing, both on the stage and in the audience. We then witnessed a beanstalk that 'grew' before our eyes with a lot of verbal encouragement from Garden Club members in the audience. And finally a giant who became so kind he volunteered to pay everyone's Poll Tax! This proved to be the last pantomime, following the death of Jack - a modest man of great talent who will be long remembered.

And so the years passed and many historical moments were made part of our Institute. In 1953 the annual outing was a trip to London to view the Coronation decorations. Some years later a slide show was given covering the funeral of Sir Winston Churchill. The year 1965 was our 21st birthday and we celebrated with a party, an iced cake and glasses of sherry provided by President, Mrs Amy Hayter. Mrs Hayter was famous for her cakes and provided delicious scones for our monthly meetings for many years. Also in the 1960s Mrs Ayers was selected by members to attend the WI's Golden Jubilee Party at Buckingham Palace.

The 1980s, with Doris Hinton as President, saw the start of the Art Group led by Mrs Penny Hawkes and several exhibitions were held. The Art Group still meets every fortnight under the guidance of Gordon Meadowcroft.

Our speakers now covered technical subjects like microwave ovens and running repairs to plugs, switches, etc. Our minds were stretched with talks on overseas travel covering the whole world. We still made donations to worthy causes, including Salisbury Cathedral Spire Appeal. One item that took place at every meeting was the presentation of birthday posies as members' birthdays arrived. These were made by Mrs Phyl Rabbitts, who also made beautiful flower arrangements and spectacular cakes for all of our special events.

By now the 1990s were approaching and it became very hard to encourage a younger age group to join our Institute. Our President, Barbara Ellis, asked for suggestions and the times of meetings were brought forward to accommodate school hours, a 'Grannies' group was started to read to playgroup children and small children were welcomed with their mothers, but still the membership did not increase.

The 1990s seemed to fly past. A pancake race became an annual event and was even shown on local television. June 1992 saw the sale of the old Village Hall and in November 1992 we held our first meeting in the new building. This was a wonderful event as the WI had worked so hard to raise funds for the enterprise.

And so to 1995 when it became sadly obvious that our Institute had reached a point where no members were prepared to take office; at our AGM in November 1996 our Institute was suspended. Some 52 years of working together, helping together, laughing together came to an end. It was a record that a small village in Dorset can be proud of, a record that has not really ended because, soon after the end of the WI, a new club rose from the ashes: the Pimperne Mid-week Club. This time, however, with a modern outlook, men as well as women were welcomed. What a good way to start the lead up to the millennium.

Right: *Certificate of Merit awarded to Pimperne WI Savings Group, 1944.*

Above: *50th Anniversary of VE Day, 1995 - the last year for Pimperne WI.*

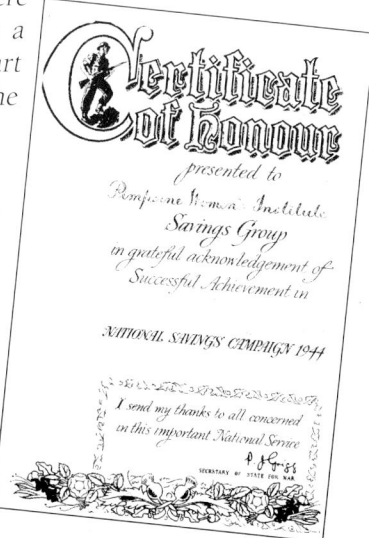

THE FLOWER SHOW

Flower Show, 1947. Photograph includes: Mrs Taylor, Mrs Pike, Mrs Cooke, Mrs Fletcher, Mrs Hall, Mrs Alner, Mrs Ridout, Mrs Vincent, Mrs North.

Above: *The first Flower Show in the new Village Hall. Jean Coull and Betty Ryland helping to set up.*

Right: *Mrs Dennis and Mrs Rabbitts admire the entries at the 1990 Flower Show.*

The Flower Show

Success of Village Show

Attractive Display at Pimperne

Full List of Winners

A baby show, a parade of decorated bicycles and prams, excerpts in the open-air from Shakespeare's "As You Like It," and selections by the band of the 1st Battalion Dorsetshire Regiment, were among the attractions of the annual produce and flower show, arranged by the Pimperne Women's Institute, in the Rectory Garden on Wednesday last week. The proceeds were shared between W.I. funds and the Dorset Regiment War Memorial Fund, which aims at realising at least £2,000 in the Blandford rural district towards the provision of a house.

The flower and produce show attracted considerably more entries than last year, and the judges had nothing but praise for the quality of the exhibits. There were also some outstanding entries in the handicraft section.

The arrangements were made by the Institute Committee, with Mrs. Melhuish as chairman, Mrs. Doris Richards as hon. treasurer, and Mrs. Wheeler, hon. secretary. The opening ceremony was undertaken by Mrs. Pass, chairman of the handicrafts section of the Dorset Federation of Women's Institutes, who paid tribute to the many willing helpers. There were stalls and competitions, among those in charge being Mrs. Taylor and Mrs. Udall (handicrafts), Mrs. Cook, Mrs. Stickland, Mrs. Port and Mrs. Smith (produce), Mrs. Small and Mrs. Hounsome (bring and buy), Mrs. Taylor and Mrs. Alner (hoop-la), Mrs. Ridout (competitions), Mrs. Wellen (bran tub), Mrs. Ellis and Mrs. Hall (ice-creams), Mrs. Miles, Mrs. Candy, Mrs. Raymond and helpers (teas), Mrs. Henderson and Mrs. Tarr (minerals), Mrs. Richards (buried treasure), and Mr. Brown and Mr. Taylor (bowling for a pig). Mr. Hawkins and helpers were on the gate.

The show was judged by Miss Dixon and Mrs. Harvey (jams), Mrs. Pass (handicrafts), and Miss Bell (flowers and vegetables). Most of the produce was Dutch auctioned by Major L. Cherry and Mrs. Melhuish.

BABY SHOW WINNERS

Dr. G. B. Forge and Nurse Hawkins judged the baby show, the winners being:—Under six months—1, Robert Taylor; 2, Yvonne Henderson; extra prizes, Brian John Brett and Pauline Cornick. Over six months—1, Stephen Gothard; 2, Terence Ridout. Over 12 months—1, John Bankes; 2, Margaret and Ruth Bailey; v.h.c., Richard North, Leslie Langdown and Sonia Gray. The decorated bicycles and perambulators were judged by Miss Weinholt, Mrs. Woodhouse, and Mrs. Coats, and the winners were Alan Coombs, Mary Collier, Tony Ellis and Jane Melhuish.

The selections by the Regimental band were greatly enjoyed, and in the evening the beautiful grounds made a perfect background for scenes for "As You Like It," given by members of the Pimperne W.I. with the help of members of the Blandford W.I., and produced by Miss Munn. Shakespearean songs were effectively sung by a small choir under Mrs. A. V. Winsor. Attractive country dances and songs were given by members of the Sixpenny Handley W.I. who presented a song scena, in costume, "Come to the fair."

The Rector (Rev. C. L. Richards) thanked all those who had taken part, especially Dr. and Mrs. Forge and the Handley players, and congratulated the W.I. on the successful manner in which the show had been organised. Mrs. Melhuish voiced the Institute's thanks to the Rector and Mrs. Richards for the use of the Rectory gardens.

At the invitation of Mr. and Mrs. C. Coats, an open-air dance was held on the lawn of Hyde Farm

Left: *Flower Show in the old Village Hall, 1986. Included in the picture are Mrs Farrell and Mrs Rayment.*

Left and above: *Cuttings from local newspapers on the success of Pimperne Show. The above cutting comes from the* Poole & Dorset Herald *dated 24 July 1947.*

THE BOOK OF PIMPERNE

The Garden Club at Bowleaze Cove, 1990s.

*Garden Club Members enjoy a hayride, August 1985.
Included in the photograph are: Lily Barnett, Win. Usher, Jack Barnett, Les Usher, Joan Bateman, Frank Saunders, Fred Waterman, Ron Hughes, Grace Abbey, Pam Howard, Margaret Trotman, Gladys Puckett.*

GROUPS, SHOWS AND CELEBRATIONS

The Garden Club

The Garden Club was started in 1970 by Mrs Marjory Fuller (*left*), with Mr Bert Lewin as Secretary. Over the years membership has flourished and so have the gardens, with Jack Barnett's store providing seeds and garden supplies to members. Fred Waterman and Jean Coull (as Treasurer and Secretary) have organised the social events, many of which have become a regular part of the village year – the fish-and-chip lunch in February, Sunday lunch at Bowleaze Cove in October, summer coach trips and the annual Christmas party.

The first of the very popular Gardens Open Weekends was held in July 1990 with 24 members opening their gardens on a very hot summer weekend. The event raised over £400 for the new Village Hall fund – £98 of which was made from the sale of tea to the thirsty visitors!

The Flower Shows, organised jointly with the WI caused immense interest and not a little rivalry. Ted Hayter and Frank Saunders were great village characters and great friends – the poem overleaf was read at the Christmas Concert that year, 1987 (at a time when the Rector's popularity was not as high as it might have been, due to a dispute over the ownership of the old Village Hall).

Above: *Visit to the Gardens of Cornwall, 1997. Millie Waterman, Lily Barnett, Doris and Peter Duncan, Nancy Brickell, Jean Coull, Fred Waterman.*
Top: *Fish-and-chip lunch, February 1990. Left table: Ron and Ivy Hughes, Gladys Pucket, Hilda and Arthur Martin; Phyllis Gulbins is at the head of the right-hand table, Kitty Keane stirs raffle tickets.*

THE MARROW
by Fred Waterman with apologies to G. Oakley

Some had fatter turmuts and some had redder beet,
Some had bigger tiddies or gurt big ears of wheat.
Some had clumps of rhubarb as high as village cross,
But they'll never whack Ted's marrow, cos 'e's thirty foot across

Frank's face turned black as thunder when he saw 'en in the cart.
'Twere the biggest one 'e'd ever sid and the sight near broke his heart,
'E turned quite queer, 'is temper flared, 'is nose went all aglow,
'E swore 'e'd grow a bigger one come next year's Flower Show.

So 'e put in forty rows of seed and stood guard every night.
'Twere 'e wot brought Doc David out when they got a touch of blight.
As 'e watched they rows for rabbits you could hear his old gun roar
We never went down Arlecks Lane in case Frank's aim were poor.

He was stretched out fast asleep one night when summat moved close by,
He grabbed his gun from off his lap and let the hammer fly.
Too late he sid his toe were there as 'e let go wi both barrels
And his howls they woke Ted Hayter up as he hopped amongst they marrows.

Now Barbara she went wild at this and when the moon did shine
She pinched his marrows, all but one, and made them into wine.
The one she left Frank watched with care and gave it rapt attention,
Fed it all the book prescribed and things I dare not mention.

Well all went quiet till Flower Show time, the day dawned bright and sunny,
Frank cut the marrow at break of day and polished it with honey.
To get the marrow to the hall took six good men and true
And half of they were ruptured before the job were through.

Ted took one look and shook his head 'taint going through thic door,
The jamb be three foot two across, the marrow's six foot four.
So Jack came up to have a look to see what 'twas all about
'E said 'You'd better leave it yer, I'll bring the judges out.'

The Parson came from in the hall and shouted out 'Well Done!'
We saw the pin on thic rosette and turned around to run.
They heard the bang at Blandford Camp, 'twere the very thing we'd feared
We found a collar on the ground, but his dog had disappeared.

We thought we'd lost the Parson too but then we heard 'en shout,
E'd landed in the pigsty and the pigs 'ad flung 'en out.
They still tell of thick marrow when pub lights start to flicker
But there idn a Flower Show no more, 'cause the hall went with the vicar!

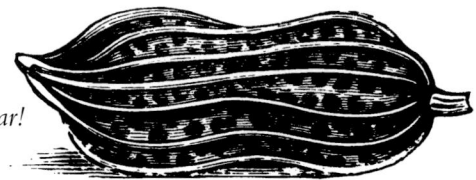

GROUPS, SHOWS AND CELEBRATIONS

The Camera Club at Sturminster Newton Mill, 1995.

THE CAMERA CLUB

The Camera Club started in the 1970s, holding monthly meetings throughout the winter and putting the skills acquired to good use on summer walks. They have produced some outstanding results. Over the years Rick Ellis, as Chairman, has compiled an invaluable and well-documented photographic record of the village. John Dowdeswell, as *Western Gazette* correspondent, has also compiled two volumes of press cuttings covering village events and in due course both of these collections will go to the County Archives to provide a permanent record of our times.

THE MID-WEEK CLUB

The Mid-week Club was started in the 1970s by Mrs Farquharson Roberts and flourished for several years, the presentation of Betty Penny's 'Cavalcade of Costume' in the Old Rectory being one of their memorable events. The Club lapsed for some years but re-started in a different form following the demise of the WI. The new Mid-week Club is open to everyone and has an interesting programme of speakers and outings.

THE LUNCH CLUB

The Lunch Club is open to anyone of any age living in the village and aims to provide companionship and a good two-course lunch with tea or coffee for £2. The meal is prepared and served every Thursday by the Probation Service using Community Service workers.

The village school provides musical entertainment each term, a useful meeting point across the generations which is much enjoyed by young and old alike. Occasional coach trips to Swanage, West Bay or the New Forest are popular with members.

PIMPERNE BADMINTON CLUB

Pimperne Badminton Club was one of the many organisations that sprang up after the new Village Hall opened; until then there had been no adequate facility for the sport, but the spacious dimensions of the new building, including the high ceiling, meant that a court could be marked out and badminton played regularly every Thursday evening.

The Club is not affiliated to any league, members come simply for the fun and exercise and comprise all ages and standards of play. Those not on the court have a coffee and a chat, so it is a pleasant social evening. Recently a junior section has been formed for 8-12-year-olds earlier in the evening, thus extending the playing time and encouraging the young people of the village to indulge in some healthy exercise.

PIMPERNE SHORT MAT BOWLING CLUB

Pimperne Short Mat Bowling Club was also set up when the new Village Hall opened in 1993, with Malcolm Reed as the first Chairman and the help of the Parish Council in obtaining grants to purchase the first mats. The Club has gone from strength to strength ever since and there is even a waiting list for membership.

For many years there have been weekly step aerobic classes and yoga classes, both well attended. Pictured here is the yoga group which includes: Joyce Honnor, Barbara Ellis, Beryl Kaile, Gwen ?, Stephanie Beggs, ?, Beryl ?, Madge ?, Irene Dowdeswell.

A small group of writers with a wide spread of talent hold monthly meetings in the village; they are pictured here with their latest anthology. Left to right: Robin Clarke, Matti Ruck, David Wheeler, Barbara Ellis, Len Scott, Anne Allan, Libby Clowes, Barry Mullender.

GROUPS, SHOWS AND CELEBRATIONS

New Mid-week Club on Poole Harbour, July 1995. Included are: Eric Ryland, Di Bozie, Peter and Doris Duncan, Mary Moores and Connie Johnston, Barbara and Rick Ellis, Janet Parker, Brenda Roberts.

Children from the school entertain the Lunch Club, 1997.
Left to right: Emma Bartlett, Sapphire Pierrepont, ?, Gabriel Reynolds, Oliver Griffiths, Angus Hogg, Harriet Bryant, Ryan Glover, Jennifer Thomas, Jonathan Percival.
Anne Cunniffe, headteacher, is seated.

*The Camera Club at Sturminster Newton Mill, 1995.
Included are: Gordon Meadowcroft, Tony Penny, Anne and daughters, Chris McCall, Beryl Kaile, Andy, Cyril Ball Ivor Mullins, Jack Antell, Sylvia Mullins.*

Cavalcade of Costume at the Old Rectory, 1970s. Included are: Pat Hunt, Jean Maidment, Betty Cochrane, Anne Biles, Doreen Edwards, Nancy Williams, Bridget Jelks and Mrs Penny's models.

GROUPS, SHOWS AND CELEBRATIONS

Pimperne Short Mat Bowling Club, 1999.
Left to right, back: Len Langdon, Gordon Crabtree, Bernie ?, Mike Hamnett, Ernie Pink, Cyril and Win Ball, Peter Duncan;
front: Barbara Langdon, Kevin Donaldson, Win Usher, Julie Hamnett, John Ridout, Sylvia Pink, Beryl Ridout, Chris McCall.

Badminton Club, 2000. Included are: Richard White, Peter Brind and Graham Jenner.

The Old Reading Room (Men's Club) for sale, May 2000.

*Pimperne Men's Club, 1998.
Left to right, back: Peter Duncan, Cyril Ball, Jack Barnett, Ken Honnor, Fred Waterman, ?;
front: Peter Yorke, Roy Adam, John Prater, Lt Col M. Oliver.*

GROUPS, SHOWS AND CELEBRATIONS

Pimperne Youth Club Rounders Team, 1954.
Left to right, back: Reg Joyce, D. Rayment, A. Dennis, P. Mullins, B. Sturmey, J. Wolmington; middle: Thelma Pope, Stella Langdown, B. Fripp, B. Tarr, M. Langdown, B. Taylor; front: P. Osment, J. Langdown, N. Towning.

Youth Club AGM, October 1989. Left to right, back: John Blake, Muriel Davis, Fred Waterman, Peter Slocombe, Jean Coull, Suzanne Green, Mark Dowse, Peter Boyt, Patrick Quinne and Jon Crabtree; seated: Mark Hinton, Richard Boyt, Barry and Coleen Walbridge (leaders) Sarah Gosney, Kerry Turner & Barbara Ellis (Chairman). Seated on floor: Francis Randerson and Mark Hatcher.

Brown Owl, Mrs Taylor and her Brownies, 1962.

Parent/Toddler Group in the new Village Hall, 2000.

GROUPS, SHOWS AND CELEBRATIONS

Pimperne Men's Club

Pimperne Men's Club bought the Old Reading Room from the Portman Estates in 1924 for £150 and for many years it flourished as a meeting place for a game of billiards or darts and to catch up on the village news. The Club lapsed in the 1960s and the building was used intermittently by the Brownies and Youth Club, but without proper maintenance became very run down. In 1997 the Men's Club was re-formed under the chairmanship of John Prater and the decision was taken to sell the building - the proceeds to go to the Parish Council to be used for the benefit of the village.

Play Schools

Play Schools have come a long way since the first one was started in the old Village Hall in the 1970s with a few toys, crayons and building bricks and present playleaders must look back wistfully to pre-OFSTED days. However, they have faced the challenge and achieved excellent results. Successive play leaders have made an outstanding contribution in giving our children a sound and happy base on which to build. The fact that the village is relatively free from youth vandalism is due in no small way to the sense of belonging engendered by these early years and continued in the village school. It is impossible to overestimate their importance.

Parent/Toddler Group

Parent/Toddler Group provides a meeting point for parents with babies and younger children, often a time when it is easy to feel isolated, especially in country areas. Up to 50 meet on Wednesday mornings in the Village Hall where toys and activities are provided for the children while parents enjoy a cup of coffee and a chat.

Pimperne Brownies

Pimperne Brownies were started in the 1950s by Mrs Taylor, a teacher at the school who lived in Portman Road, who often held meetings in her garden when they were not held in the Old Reading Room. There has been a thriving membership ever since, with Mrs Jo Banks as the current Brown Owl.

Above and top: Toddlers at play with their mums at the Parent/Toddler Group.

Blandford Machine Knitting Group

Not for needles and patterns
And small woolly balls
With a jumper each month if you try.
No – machines had arrived
And a row could be knitted
With a whoosh... in the wink of an eye.

When Pimperne's Village Hall was built the
group decided to move
And once a month
The ladies arrive
With Toyota, knitmaster and Brother,
Coming to grips
With computers and cards,
All offering help to each other.

With Dot in the Chair, and Win taking cash,
and Secretary Jean sorting 'things'
Each meeting's a joy
Till a machine makes a bang –
Then stops – and a hush fills the hall.
Then 'all hands to the pump'
To look for the fault
(and sometimes a husband to call).

So the years have sped by, and the talent has
grown, with garments of outstanding beauty
From shawls for the babies
To cardies for teens,
Skirts, suits and tops for the rest.
All articles worn
With such pride for it's known
That the Knitting Group fashions are best.

by Connie Johnston

Left to right, back: Pat Hill, Jean Welling, Annabel Glasspool, Doris Holman, Rosemary Rose, front: Lucy Mower, Nora Beck, Winn Ball, Olive Davies.

Coronation party in the old Village Hall, 1953. Included in the picture at the back are: Mrs Hounsome, Mrs Vincent, Mrs Lucas, Desmond Tuckett; back seated: Mrs Candy, Mr Wilson, Fred Joyce; front seated: Mrs Wilson and Mr Bavington; standing right front: Stella Langdown; standing at back: Jack Thorne, Cdr and Mrs Buckle and Revd Foxhall Smedley.

GROUPS, SHOWS AND CELEBRATIONS

THE VILLAGE FÊTE *(by Roy Adam)*

Villages used to have an inward look, people were concerned almost exclusively with affairs in the immediate neighbourhood. Before the coming of TV people largely had to make their own fun, particularly in villages where there was a closely interwoven pattern of life and neighbourliness. Those who remember life in the 1930s will agree we got much more pleasure in making our own entertainment.

The annual fête was the highlight of village life, a pleasing demonstration of co-operation of young and old, rich and poor combining readily in light-hearted activities. Everybody knew everybody and great enthusiasm accompanied the proceedings. Mrs Fuge's daughter Thelma would be 'zinging s'm zongs', Mrs Newberry's son Ken 'be doin z'm rezitations'. Lloyd Stickley 'e be playing onse zummit on 'is carnet'.

The fête was held in the grounds of the Rectory and was the result of many committee meetings held during the winter months, usually under the chairmanship of the Rector.

The day arrived and in the early morning stalls were prepared, the horse and cart driven by Sheddy Hall arriving with the long boards which fitted together to form the skittle alley, the main source of income - the prize for which, a live pig, was kept in by straw bales provided by Charles Coats. The Rectory lawn was a blaze of bunting and flags of the commonwealth and a huge Union Jack.

The fête was opened by a local dignitary; I well remember the Countess of Shaftesbury and Miss Wienholt declaring the fête open and being followed by a large gathering of children. The charge was 3d. and 1d. for children.

At the back of the lawn the Blandford Town Band played under the baton of Fred Walters, an ironmonger in the town, other musical interludes being given by the Pimperne Mouth Organ Band headed by Jock Wilson, George Rayment and Harold Legg and the bellringers performing with the hand bells; I would dearly love to know what happened to them, they were the property of St Peter's Church.

During the afternoon the children took part in sports, followed by the fancy-dress competition, judged by whoever opened the fête assisted by Mrs Mabel Coats, small money prizes being given to each class by age group. For the men there was a marathon usually of one to two miles starting from the Rectory and going towards Foxwarren across to the Long Barrow and home.

During the early evening the 16-20 age group presented a play on the lawn. The large yew bushes formed a half circle with a break about 6 feet from each end, creating a first-class entrance for going on stage and leaving. I well remember one play centred on South Africa with my brother, now in his eighties, in a light grey suit and topee.

The young ladies of the village looked exquisite, maybe that was why the organisers never had difficulty getting actors. The play was produced by Mrs Gertrude Fuge, the school headteacher, a very strict disciplinarian who demanded perfection. The day ended with a dance on the lawn and I quote:

An' then at cloze, we'd make a ring
An' shout 'God save our Grashus King'.
An' whomward toddle, vree vroom ceare
Aven had the best day o'th'yer.
God grant the' day may niver cum
Wen we cain't ave our bit o'vun
At our Village Feate.

A 1940s Village Fête.

Fêtes and Celebrations

Left: *Sue Simmons and Ruth Blake lead the Fancy Dress Parade (1990 Fête).*

Below: *Gwen Dowling (gipsy), Mrs Voss (clown) and Mrs Pride (Dutch lady) at the Coronation celebrations, 1937.*

Above: *Harry Dominey as Tramp.*

Right: *Mrs A.D. Adam with Gwen Dowling and Mrs Pride at the rear of Manor House.*

134

Fêtes and Celebrations

Left: *Old Tyme Fête in Old Rectory Garden, 1990. Included are: Nancy Brickell, Connie Johnston, Kay Knight, Dorothy Bealing, Barbara Ellis, Peter Slocombe.*

Below: *Old Tyme Fête at Chestnut Farm, 1991. Mrs Betty Penny, of Cavalcade of Costume fame, with Fred Waterman and Jean Coull.*

Left: *The 1964 Village Fête in the field opposite the Farquharson Arms (now Parr Grove). Participating in the Fancy Dress are: Rachel Pollard, Rosalyn Kaile and Christine Coull.*

Below: *Dancing to the Hambledon Hopsteps at the 1990 Village Fête.*

Royal Occasions

The Jubilee of King George V and Queen Mary in 1935, and the Coronation of George VI and Queen Elizabeth in 1937 gave rise to great celebrations throughout the land. Roy Adam has preserved the accounts and minutes of Pimperne's Celebration Committee, kept by his father, Frederick Adam who was Secretary to the committee, which was chaired by Brigadier General Stuart. They make fascinating reading, the programme was as follows:

10 A.M.
UNITED SERVICE IN THE CHURCH
(COLLECTION FOR BLANDFORD HOSP.)
EACH CHILD TO BE PRESENTED WITH A MUG
(7/6D. PER DOZEN).
FOOTBALL MATCH BETWEEN MARRIED AND SINGLE
SPORTS
TREASURE HUNT ORGANISED BY MRS FUGE

4 P.M.
TEA FOR WOMEN AND CHILDREN AND O.A.P.S
FANCY DRESS PARADE

7 P.M.
SUPPER FOR THE MEN
DANCE ARRANGED BY MR WEEKS,
THE SUM OF £1 AGREED FOR MUSICIAN

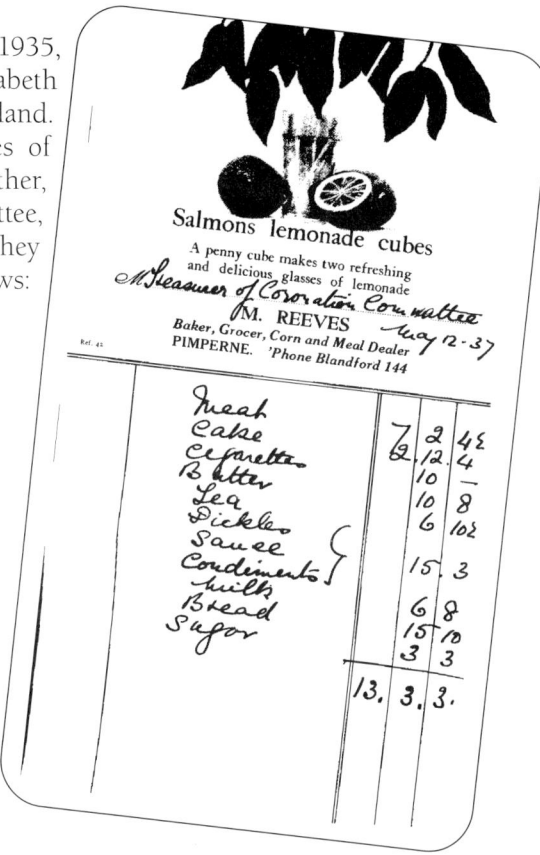

MRS BRIDGE EXPRESSED THE HOPE THAT MR NEWBURY MIGHT FIX AN AMPLIFIER TO BROADCAST THE KING'S SPEECH.

Mr F. Adam reported that any Parishioner who, through infirmity or sickness, was unable to attend the celebrations would be provided for: in the case of men tobacco or cigarettes and for women tea.

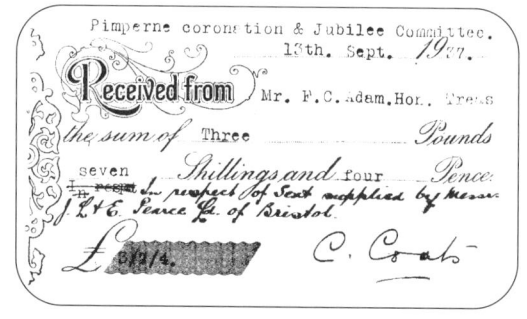

Left: *A receipt given to the Pimperne Coronation Committee to cover the cost of providing six dozen mugs and for four broken glasses - £2.6s.2d., 20 May 1937.*

Above: *Receipt for the cost of a seat supplied to the Coronation and Jubilee Committee, 1937.*

Top: *A receipt for foodstuffs from M. Reeves, '37.*

Royal Occasions

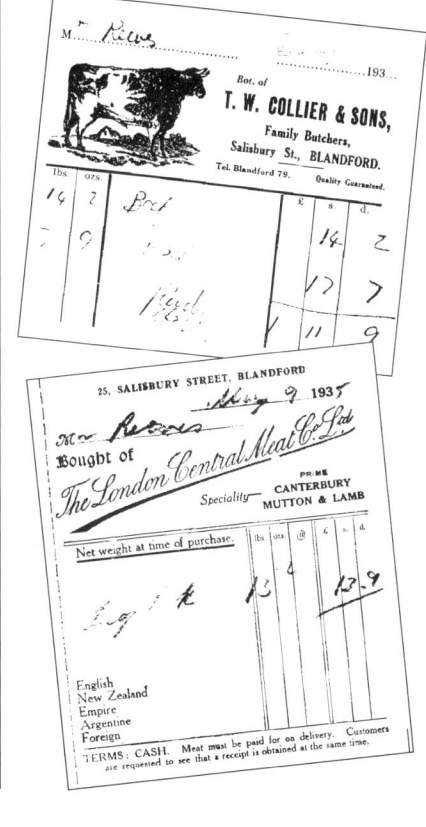

Above: *Balance sheet for the Jubilee celebrations, 10 May 1935.*

Left: *Receipt from T.W. Collier & Sons for beef to feed the revellers during the Coronation celebrations.*

Below left: *A similar receipt from The London Central Meat Co. Ltd. for lamb.*

Far left: *Receipt from M. Reeves for various foodstuffs, including mustard and salt.*

THE BOOK OF PIMPERNE

*Pimperne Cricket Club, 1968, outside the pavilion at Langbourne.
Left to right, back: John Miles, ?, ?, ?, Micky White, ?, Paddy Drennan;
front: Steve Waterman, Geoff Pike, Kevern Langdown, Timmy Stevens, Tom Barnett.*

*Pimperne Cricket Team, 1996. Left to right, back: Kevin Langdown, Matthew Glavin,
Gary Manson, Barry Hitchen, Rob Cole, Graham Langdown, Mark Birchall;
front: John Sullivan, Paul McCann, Owen Newton, Chris Langdown, Ray Hatchard, Gary Lacey.*

Chapter 9
Pimperne Sports Society

by G. Wicks with contributions from D. Griffin, R. Joyce and K. Neale

Throughout the 20th century both football and cricket played a big part in village life with many well-remembered village characters taking part. Graham Wicks, Secretary of the Sports Society, looks back to earlier days and reviews the events leading to the achievement of Priory Field.

From the early 1920s, football was played in the field opposite where the new Village Hall now stands, but the village cricket teams played at venues outside the immediate village area and on occasions these venues depended on the goodwill of local land-owners, so from year to year it was difficult for the sports clubs to make long-term plans. In addition these fields never had the luxury of a full-time groundsman as is the case with Priory Field. One of the early venues was Langbourne, owned by Major R.V. Garton. When his daughter died, Major Garton donated a sum of money towards the famous concrete wicket, which was put down in her memory, and with its hessian matting cover provided a fast but true wicket – an early version of the present 'all weather wicket'. However, the bounce on this wicket was reported to be something rather special! For years at Langbourne the teas were served by Ann and Reg Dennis, Reg being Major Garton's gardener.

The highlight of the year's cricket fixtures at Langbourne was the game against Hall & Woodhouse, when G.S.E. Woodhouse, former Somerset Captain, played for the brewery. Pimperne always thought that if he could be dismissed cheaply, Pimperne would be in with a good chance of winning. One year Mr Woodhouse came in with a brand new bat to go with the new ball which Pimperne always provided. First ball brought forth a huge appeal for 'leg before wicket'. Pimperne's umpire, Henry Pike, raised his finger and Mr Woodhouse walked, but on passing Tom Barnett, said 'have a look at my bat Tom' and there, just below the splice, was a red ring, but Mr Woodhouse continued to walk back to the pavilion! A little different from the response one might expect from today's professionals perhaps?

From Langbourne the sports clubs moved on to the Army Camp at Blandford and remained there until the pavilion was burned to the ground, when they moved to Larksmead.

Fund-raising for a dedicated home ground commenced in earnest in the early 1980s and to formalise the business of providing and running a sports and leisure facility an association was formed of interested residents of Pimperne and outlying areas. A constitution was signed in late 1991 with the stated objective of advancing the Pimperne Sports Association by assisting in the provision of facilities for the same.

The first President of the new Association was Reg Joyce, with Allan Johnson being elected as Chairman, Thelma Joyce as Treasurer and Barry Hitchen as the first Secretary.

Various fund-raising events were held over the years to generate funds and the Committee decided to seek charitable status, so as to allow access to many national sources of funding available for sports organisations. The Association was finally granted charitable status on 2 August 1994 under the new name of Pimperne Sports Society (Reg. No. 1039918). A declaration of trust was made with the object being to:

Promote the benefits of the inhabitants of the Parish of Pimperne in Dorset, without distinction of sex or political, religious or other opinions by associating the local authorities, voluntary organisations and the inhabitants in a common effort to advance education and to provide facilities in the interests of the social welfare for recreation and leisure-time occupations with the object of improving conditions of life of the said inhabitants.

The new Pimperne Sports Society, known as the Trust and governed by its trust deed, allowed for up to six trustees to be elected to oversee the day-to-day running of the Sports Society and the

Pimperne Football Club, 1951 (taken in Old Football Field opposite the site of the new Village Hall). Manager, Jack Thorne. Left to right, back: G. Elliott, L. Joyce, R. Joyce, ?, C. Dacombe, W. Putt; front: M. Dennis, R. Upward, E. Miles, A. Lukins, B. Dacombe.

Pimperne Football Club, 1975/6. Left to right, back: M. Martin, P. Joyce, P. Scott, C. Langdown, R. Edwards, M. White, N. Sims; front: M. Vickers, K. Langdown, B. Fern, D. Natolie, J. McCall, B. Meaker.

PIMPERNE SPORTS SOCIETY

Pimperne Sports Junior Football, 2000 - the Yellow Team (5-8 years).
Left to right, back: Liz Fergani, Kerry Lacey, Adam Fergani, Hannah Manson, Christopher Mogeridge, Oliver Baker, Josh Robinson, Nick Tomlinson, John Scott;
front: Charley Lacey, James Adams, Christopher Torrance, Ryan Murrey, Tom Leigh.

Pimperne Junior Football Team, 2000 - the Red Team (9-12 years).
Left to right, back: Liz Fergani, Simon Tomlinson, Richard Ebborn, Ed Saunders, Mark Murnane, James Tapper, Peter Bellman, John Scott;
front: Dominic Way, Luke Robinson, Ben Leigh, Ashley Robins, Sean Gardiner, Tarek Fergani.

The Pavilion

Right: *Presentation of the cheque from the Lottery Sports Fund, 1996. Left to right: Maureen Johnson, Liz Batten (Lottery Sports Fund), Reg and Thelma Joyce, Barry Hitchen, Ray Hatchard and Kevin Langdown.*

Below: *Opening of the new pavilion, 18 August 1996. Included are: Allan Johnson, Thelma Joyce, Liz Batten, Barry Hitchen, Chris Langdown, Mrs Norah Taylor, Reg Joyce, Ray Hatchard.*

Below: *Mrs Norah Taylor cutting the tape with Peter Slocombe to the left and Alan Johnson to the right.*

Below left: *The newly completed building, 1996.*

PIMPERNE SPORTS SOCIETY

Pimpernalia 1998

implementation of its governing document. The first trustees elected were Allan Johnson, Thelma Joyce, Barry Hitchen, John Langdown, Kevin Langdown and Ray Hatchard. On 1 July 1994 the Trust's financial account stood at £6500, this being the funds which had been raised by the Association through the previous year's fund-raising events, sponsorship and donations. Whilst all this was taking place, the search for a suitable home for the village sports clubs was ongoing. In the early 1990s when the old Mill site was being considered for re-development, Michael Taylor offered five acres of land to be used as a sports field for the village and the conveyance to the Parish Council was finally signed in September 1992. It was agreed that the field should be leased to the Sports Society for a period of 50 years at a peppercorn rent of £5 per year and this lease was signed on 6 December 1993.

A major obstacle facing the Sports Society was the regrading of the land which sloped down from the south-west corner of the field towards the north east, later to prove a problem with water drainage, but this work was completed during May 1994. The first phase of the project, the regrading of the land, the erection of a safety fence along the north-east boundary, the seeding of the field and the laying of an artificial cricket wicket was completed in the late summer of 1995.

In September 1995 the news that the Lottery Sports Fund would make a major donation to the project meant that the construction of a pavilion could go ahead and this was completed during the early summer of 1996, with North Dorset District Council issuing a completion certificate on 5 July 1996. The main contractor for the pavilion was Martyn Lewis (building contractor) and the final cost of the project nearly £120 000. To celebrate the completion of the field and pavilion, the Sports Society arranged to hold an opening event on Sunday 18 August, 1996. The facility was officially opened by Mrs Nora Taylor and a competition to name the field was won by Sylvia Packham of Berkeley House, Church Road. Dignitaries from the Parish Council, North Dorset District Council, Dorset Playing Fields Association, Dorset County Cricket, Dorset County Football Association, along with Liz Batten of the Lottery Sports Fund Sports Council, attended to celebrate the big day and the naming of the facility 'Priory Field'.

In July 1998 the facilities were extended to include a double set of cricket practice nets and this facility was officially opened by Notts and England cricketer, Derek Randall, along with Richard Mocridge from Dorset County Cricket. Once again the project was supported by the Parish Council along with North Dorset District Council, Dorset Playing Fields Association and the Lords Taverners/ECB.

In the latter part of the 1990s the Village Church and Sports Society combined their efforts to provide a village fête which had the catching name 'Pimpernalia', and these yearly events, organised by Martin Richley and Sue Hatchard, were very successful; being well attended they raised funds for both the Parochial Church Council and the Sports Society.

The village now has a sports and leisure facility which is much envied by visiting teams from throughout Dorset Cricket and Dorset Football Associations. It is used by other local authorities as a model on which to plan similar facilities and is without doubt an outstanding achievement by all those who spent many long hours working on the project. In this respect, and like all successful organisations, the name of our secretary at that time comes to the fore as being instrumental in making the project successful – this was Barry Hitchen. One need only read through the mountain of paperwork associated with the project to understand his unceasing input and if ever a civic award were due, then Barry Hitchen would be a well deserving candidate.

Staff car and driver.
(By kind permission of Alan Harfield, courtesy of the Royal Signals Museum)

Sub. Lt. H. Starkey, Nelson Battn. R.N.D., 1915.

Chapter 10
Pimperne and the Military
with much help from Alan Harfield

Blandford Camp stands on the hill above Pimperne and has had an important influence on the village and its inhabitants for nearly 200 years.

In 1984 Alan Harfield published an intriguing and well-researched book about the camp and its immediate neighbourhood entitled *Blandford and the Military* and the book is recommended to anyone whose appetite is whetted by this chapter, much of which is based on his writings, together with considerable help from the staff of the Royal Signals Museum, where a wealth of further information can be found.

As early as the 1720s a troop of cavalry (the 7th Hussars) was stationed in the Parish of Pimperne in the area now known as Camp Down (which lies to the left of Shaftesbury Lane from Sunrise Business Park towards Stourpaine crossroads). Before the days of permanent barracks it was necessary to settle cavalry regiments for the winter months in an area where adequate cover and forage could be obtained. In Dorset, cavalry regiments were usually split into troops which were then stationed in various locations around the county, one of which was Pimperne – Camp Down was an ideal situation for a winter camp located in a dip in the downs with fresh water available at the foot of the down in the area now known as France Firs. The troop remained in the area until 1731 when it was ordered to move to Crookhome (Crewkerne) in Somerset.

One of the reasons for troops being stationed in the area at this time was to assist customs officers in the campaign against smuggling. Hampshire and Dorset were very much in the forefront of the smuggling trade. One well-known smuggling track in the area is still shown as Smugglers Lane on current editions of the Ordnance Survey map. It first appeared on a map dated 1690 when it was shown passing by Durweston to Stour-pain (Stourpaine) and Stepleton.

Unknown airman, 1919.

The troops were required to assist officers of the Customs against Owlers and Smugglers. An owler was a person guilty of the offence of carrying either wool or sheep out of the county. As the bands of smugglers grew larger it was not uncommon for them to have sizeable parties with squads of batmen, who formed escorts and provided scouting parties to move ahead of the main convoy and to have a rearguard, both keeping watch out for the Revenue men or Dragoons. Geoffrey Morley, in his book *Smuggling in Hampshire and Dorset 1700-1850* records that, as the penalty for the carrying of firearms was to suffer the death penalty, batmen were armed with large ash or holly clubs, but as the smuggling trade became more violent guns and swords and cutlasses were used.

The next unit to occupy the Camp Down site at Pimperne was a troop of the Royal Regiment of North British Dragoons in 1738. In addition to anti-smuggling, at this time troops were needed to help maintain law and order when changes in manufacturing in the Wiltshire weaving trade and the subsequent lowering of wages caused riots. In December 1738 an order was sent by express at midnight from London to the Royal Regiment of North British Dragoons ordering it to march immediately for Chippenham and the Pimperne troop joined the regiment in Warminster. The riots were suppressed by mid February, three of the ringleaders were hanged from the gallows in Salisbury and the troops returned to base.

Hunger riots followed throughout the 18th century and the Dragoons were often called out to help protect mills, markets, granaries etc. and to help break up roving bands of illegal price regulators.

With the outbreak of the Seven Year War with France in 1756 a camp was set up at Shroton Lines which, like Camp Down at Pimperne, was within marching distance of Race Down (the site of the

Despatch rider with pigeons leaving for the firing line His Majesty's Pigeon Service, November 1917.

The late Mr E.D. Horsey, a Blandford butcher, visiting the RND camp, 1917.
(By kind permission of Alan Harfield, courtesy of the Royal Signals Museum)

present Blandford Camp). Race Down provided the large area of open downland needed for reviews and manoeuvres with large numbers of troops. The *Salisbury & Winchester Journal* of 30 August 1756 records that 20 000 spectators watched the Review at Race Down when approximately 10 000 cavalry, infantry and artillery were assembled and exercised. The effect of such an event on the quiet life of Pimperne can be imagined!

During the Napoleonic Wars large numbers of barracks were constructed all over the country and this did away with the need for temporary winter quarters so that from the end of the 18th century there is no further record of any troops at the Pimperne Camp of the Cavalry.

The area that is now Blandford Camp was open downland used as a recreational area for Blandford, with a racecourse and cricket ground until the 19th century, although it was periodically used for the training of local militias from the mid-18th century.

Its first recorded permanent military use was in 1806 when the Admiralty shutter telegraph station was established. The need for fast communication between London and the naval bases led to the Admiralty commissioning the erection of chains of relay stations on hilltops from London to Portsmouth and Plymouth. One of these relay stations is recorded as having been built on a hill just over a mile east of Pimperne Church, adjacent to Blandford Racecourse (the site is now known as Telegraph Clump due to the small wood that now occupies the site).

The relay station was a two-room wooden hut with an operating room and living room-cum-kitchen. The shutter frame was fixed to the roof – stout timbers about 20 ft high which had to withstand high winds on this exposed hilltop position. In 1810 the station was manned by three civilians, they were: Philip Webb, foreman, aged 48, an ex-stocking weaver, who had been 4 years, 3 months at the station; Thomas Hill, aged 33, previous occupation husbandry, 2 years on the station and Matthew Ware, aged 21, a lame labourer, who had been 1 year, 8 months on the station.

The last two were glassmen who manned the telescopes. During the hours the stations were open the glassmen were not allowed to leave their telescopes for more than two minutes! The system was capable of passing information from originator to recipient in about ten minutes – weather conditions permitting! The operators acquired a great deal of expertise in the operation of the telegraph shutters and it is recorded that a pre-arranged signal could be communicated between London and Plymouth, via the Blandford Racecourse station, and acknowledged back, in three minutes. The chain of stations was

Trooper Walter Dowling, The Dorset Yeomanry (aged 21) during the South African War, 1900.

in use throughout the Napoleonic wars of the early-19th century.

After the Battle of Waterloo the Admiralty instructed the whole of the Establishment of Telegraphs to be immediately discontinued. The Blandford Racecourse relay station therefore became non-operational from March 1816.

The hut, together with its garden, would have been kept in a reasonable state, against the necessity of being taken into use again, until 1825 but the staff was reduced. The officer in charge was allowed to reside at the station rent-free but was responsible for all maintenance. They were usually excellent gardeners and were able to support themselves and their families with vegetables and some even kept poultry and pigs. A proposed improved scheme was being installed 1825/31 but was abandoned with the advent of the new electric telegraph system.

The Dorset Yeomanry Cavalry was first formed in 1803, due to the resumption of hostilities between Britain and France, volunteering became fashionable and the Dorset Yeomanry Cavalry assembled regularly at Camp Down until they were disbanded in 1814.

In the autumn of 1830 the situation was critical in southern counties following agricultural riots, burning of farmhouses and destruction of agricultural machinery. Dorset Yeomanry re-formed in 1831.

THE BOOK OF PIMPERNE

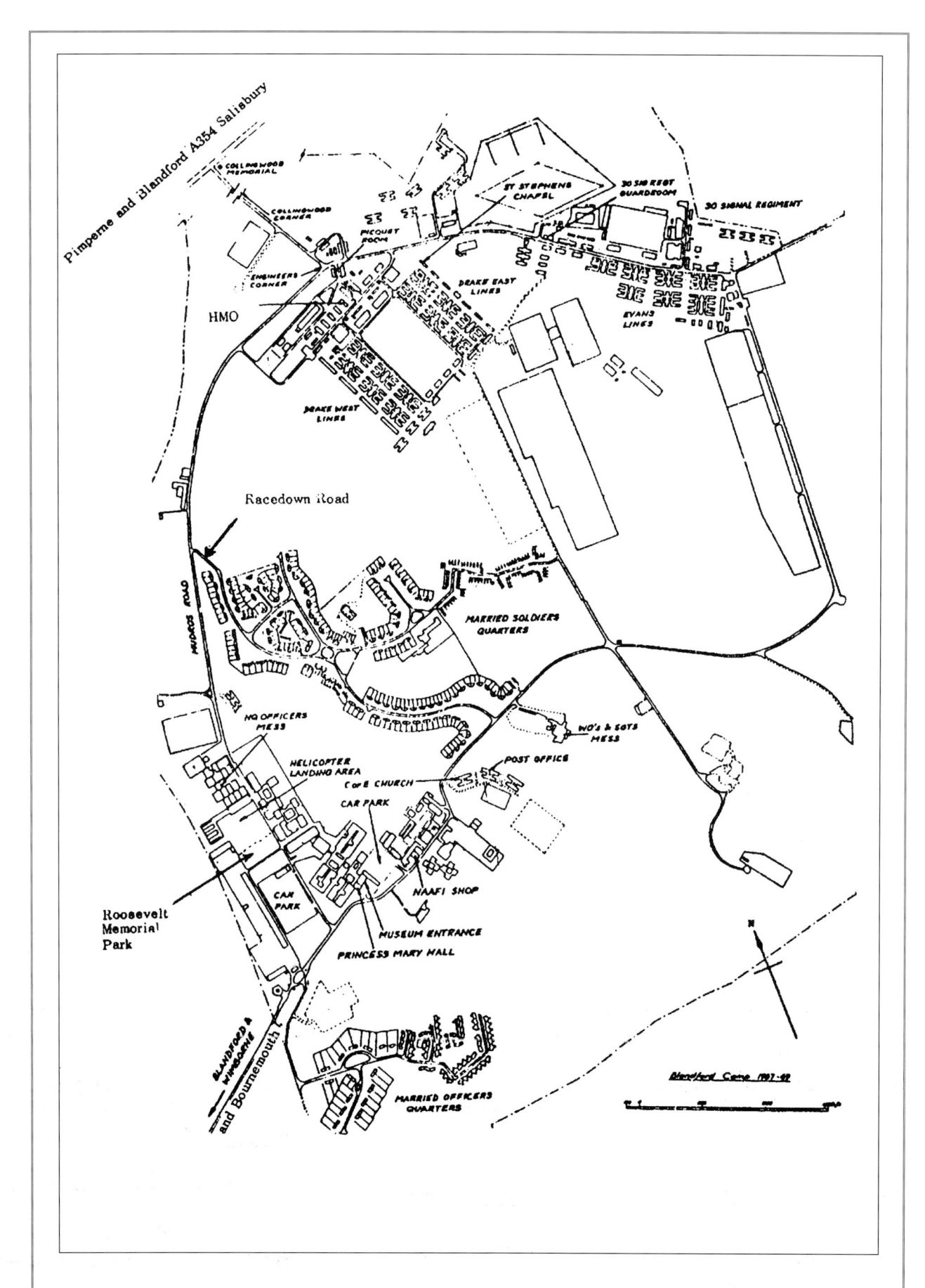

Map of Blandford Camp, 1967-69.
(By kind permission of Alan Harfield, courtesy of the Royal Signals Museum)

PIMPERNE AND THE MILITARY

Blandford Troop had four officers who were as follows:

Captain – James John Farquharson of Langton
Lieutenants – James John Farquharson (Junior) of Langton
Henry William Berkeley Portman of Bryanston
Cornet – Frederick James Farquharson of Langton

Their rather splendid uniform consisted of a red coatee faced with white, two rows of gold braid on the cuffs and collar. Dark blue trousers with one gold stripe. Crimson and gold girdle. The helmet was of brass, without a plume. The NCOs and men had a yellow braid stripe on the blue trousers instead of gold.

Unfortunately they were disbanded in March 1838 due to Government cuts and it was not until 1859 that a War Office Circular was sent to Lords Lieutenant of Counties authorising them to raise Volunteer Corps within their counties. Under this act the volunteers were expected to provide their own arms and equipment and to cover all other expenses, except if actually called out for active service. This really confined the new force to fairly well-to-do people such as tradesmen, clerks, some of the more junior professional men and better than average paid artisans, as no person receiving 19th-century labourer's pay would have been able to afford the expense involved.

The 8th Corps of the Dorset Rifle Volunteers was formed in Blandford in February 1860 and frequently trained on the Race Down which was also used by the Queen's Own Dorset Yeomanry Cavalry. In 1870 C Telegraph Troop of the Royal Engineers was formed to provide communications for the field army. At that time communications would have been either by telegraph or by visual means. The troop diary for the year shows that on 1 August 1872 half the troop, comprising 2 officers, 108 men and 82 horses took part in an army exercise at Race Down. The troop record shows: the telegraph was in use during 28 days, for 370 hours. Out of the 28 days there were 26 on which faults occurred sometimes 3 or 4 on the same day. The faults were due mostly to the cable being cut by accident or by design, on one occasion it was bitten through by a horse... The exercise lasted until 10 September. This is the first recorded visit to Blandford Race Down of any communication unit of the army and it is interesting to note that C Telegraph Troop was a forebear of the Royal Signals who were to take over Blandford in 1967.

Linesman on horseback laying cable, late-19th century.

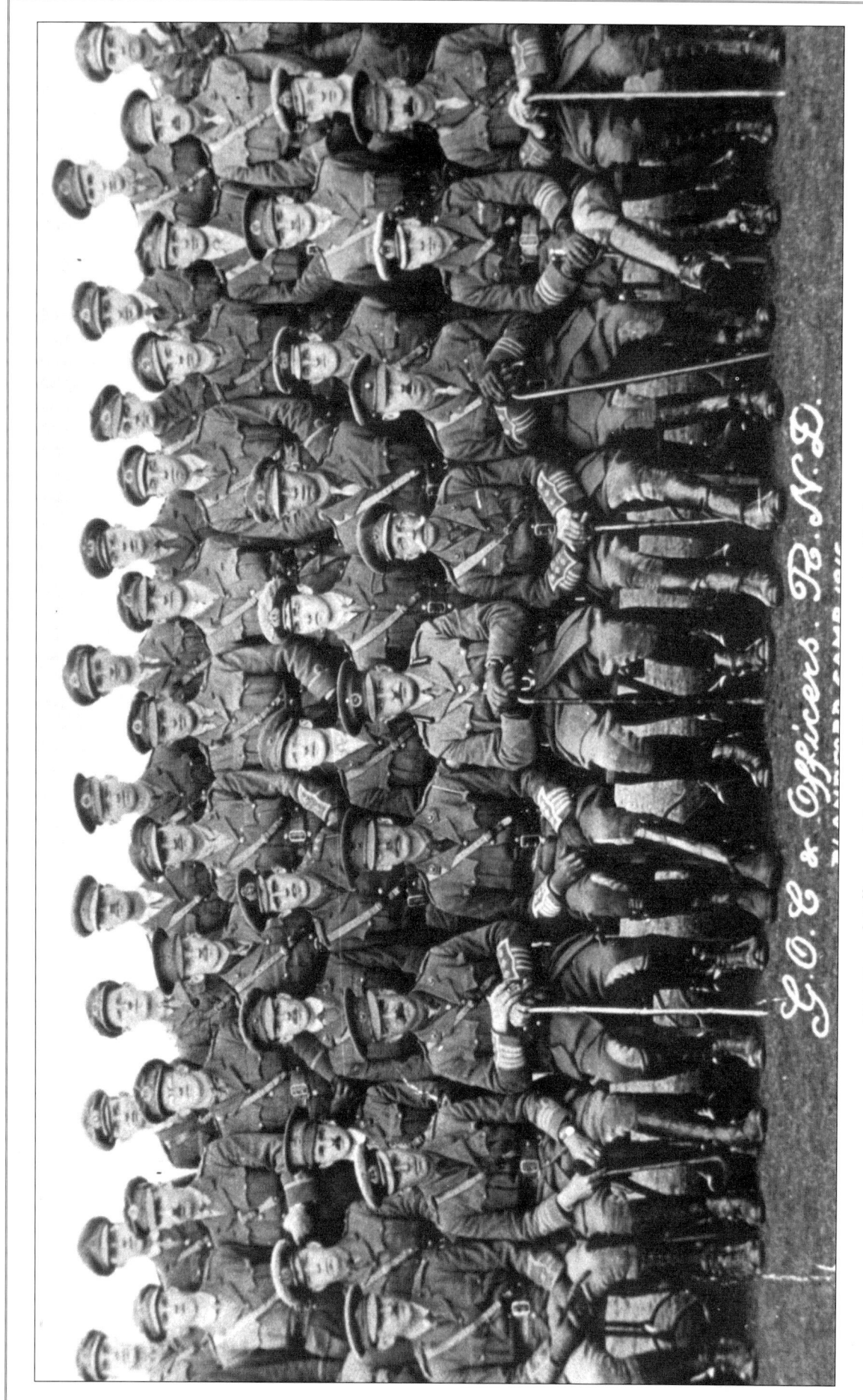

G.O.C. and Officers of the Royal Naval Division, Blandford Camp, 1916.

PIMPERNE AND THE MILITARY

THE ROYAL NAVAL DIVISION

This division was formed in 1914 from personnel serving in the Royal Naval Reserve, Royal Fleet Reserve and Royal Naval Volunteer Reserve, Royal Marines and some recruits from the Pontefract area. After some training they were moved to Belgium and were subjected to three days of bombardment and attack in the trenches in October 1914. They were able to hold the defence of Antwerp which enabled the Belgian Field Army and British Expeditionary Force to secure the channel ports. By the end of this brief engagement the Royal Naval Division had lost 7 officers and 53 men killed; 2 officers and 135 men wounded; 37 officers and 1442 men had been interned in Holland and 5 officers and 931 men were prisoners of war in Germany. Of the 700 officers and men of the Collingwood Battalion who embarked for Belgium only 22 returned to England to form the nucleus of a new Collingwood Battalion.

The Royal Naval Division was re-formed as a mobile division at the Blandford Camp, which was under construction. The first unit arrived in November 1914 and the remainder in January, those whose lines were not ready for occupation were sent into billets in houses in Pimperne, Iwerne Minster and Shillingstone. Major General Sir Archibald Parish and his staff established themselves in Stud House, Pimperne, a property that had been requisitioned for the use of the General and his staff.

The construction of Blandford Camp during the winter of 1914-15 was only achieved after numerous problems had been overcome. The timber, bricks, cement and stores had to be transported from Blandford railway station to the site via Black Lane, which at that time was merely a chalk track and the heavy steam engines with large trailers and horse drawn carts turned the lane into a mire. The lane was then paved in the worst section by the very timber required to build the camp! A lot of local labour was given temporary employment while the camp was being built.

The whole camp was made up of wooden buildings with duckboards between buildings so that men could get around without becoming covered in mud. Duckboards were familiar items to servicemen in the First World War and were part of every day life in the trenches. Blandford Camp was, because of its exposed position on the downs, considered one of the healthiest in the country. It was entirely self-contained.

The Royal Naval Division suffered enormous casualties at Gallipoli and was later engaged in the Somme and fighting at Arras and Passchendale, the years of 1915, 1916 and 1917 saw many men pass through Blandford, they came as replacement for the many casualties that the Division suffered in the actions in which it was engaged.

The training at Blandford Camp commenced in adverse winter conditions in 1914-1915 with the camp being referred to as a sea of mud - this changed to problems with intense heat in the following summer. It is recorded that the men of each battalion were given concentrated training including drills, exercises on Blandford downs, acting as defence units for mock attacks on Pimperne village. Trenches like those in France were dug on the slopes above and to the left of Stud House and stormed in mock attacks.

The Royal Naval Division existed for only five years and in 1919 passed into the pages of Naval and Military History. At the final parade at Horse Guards Parade on 6 June 1919 they were inspected by HRH the Prince of Wales who addressed them as follows:

Fredk. Adam, R.N.D., married Amy Dowling from the Farquharson Arms, Pimperne, 1915.

It is a great pleasure to me to see you all here today and it is a privilege to inspect you on parade. More than four years have passed since the King at Blandford Camp inspected the Royal Naval Division on the occasion of your departure for the Dardanelles. Since then the story of the war has unfolded itself and, after many vicissitudes and disappointments, strange turns and changes of fortune, the complete victory of our arms, and of our cause, has in every quarter of the World been attained. In all this you have borne a part which bears comparison with the record of any Division in the Armies of the British Empire. In every theatre of war, your military conduct has been exemplary. Whether on the slopes of Achi Baba, or on the Somme, or in the valley of the Ancre, or down to the very end at the storming of the Hindenburg Line, your achievements have been worthy of the best traditions both of the Royal Navy and the British Army.

There are few here today of those to whom the King bade farewell in February 1915. Some who

THE BOOK OF PIMPERNE

> YOU ARE ABOUT TO BECOME A SOLDIER. This will mean a big change in your life. You will find yourself performing unfamiliar duties in a new atmosphere.
>
> At first, naturally, you will feel rather strange to your surroundings: you will miss your home and friends. But you will soon realise that your comrades are in the same position, and that you are all starting from the same mark.
>
> Later, when you have grown more familiar with your duties, and the reasons at the back of these duties, you will realise something else—namely, the greatness of the service which you are to-day rendering to your country; a service which that country will always gratefully remember.
>
> Here are three words of advice :—
>
> (1) Learn to obey all orders smartly and without question. This is not a mere matter of outward show: very often the lives of an entire body of men may depend upon the prompt action of a single individual. The more thoroughly you acquire that habit the safer you and those who serve with you will be, and the sooner we shall achieve final victory and peace.
>
> (2) Acquaint yourself with the traditions of your particular corps or unit, and live up to them. This will lead you to take a pride in its history, and will foster in you the team-spirit, commonly known as *esprit de corps* which is the life-blood of the soldier.
>
> (3) The British Army draws peculiar strength from the close relations which have always existed between officers and men. The officer's first duty is to his men: he not only leads them into action, but he is responsible for their welfare and comfort at other times. He joins in their games, he listens to their troubles. Therefore, whenever you stand in need of aid or advice, do not hesitate to approach him (through your serjeant or other non-commissioned officer) and tell him the whole story.
>
> Once more I welcome you to the Army. Fear God, Honour the King, and May Victory Soon Crown Our Arms !
>
> THE WAR OFFICE   *Anthony Eden*   Secretary of State for

Left: *Message from Anthony Eden given to recruits arriving at the Camp in 1939.*

Below and left: *Certificates for wages paid to Prisoners of Wars 1917 and 1918.*

Below: *Account for horses and carts as the camp prepares for mobilisation June 1939.*

Certificate of POW Wages 9.6.1918

152

PIMPERNE AND THE MILITARY

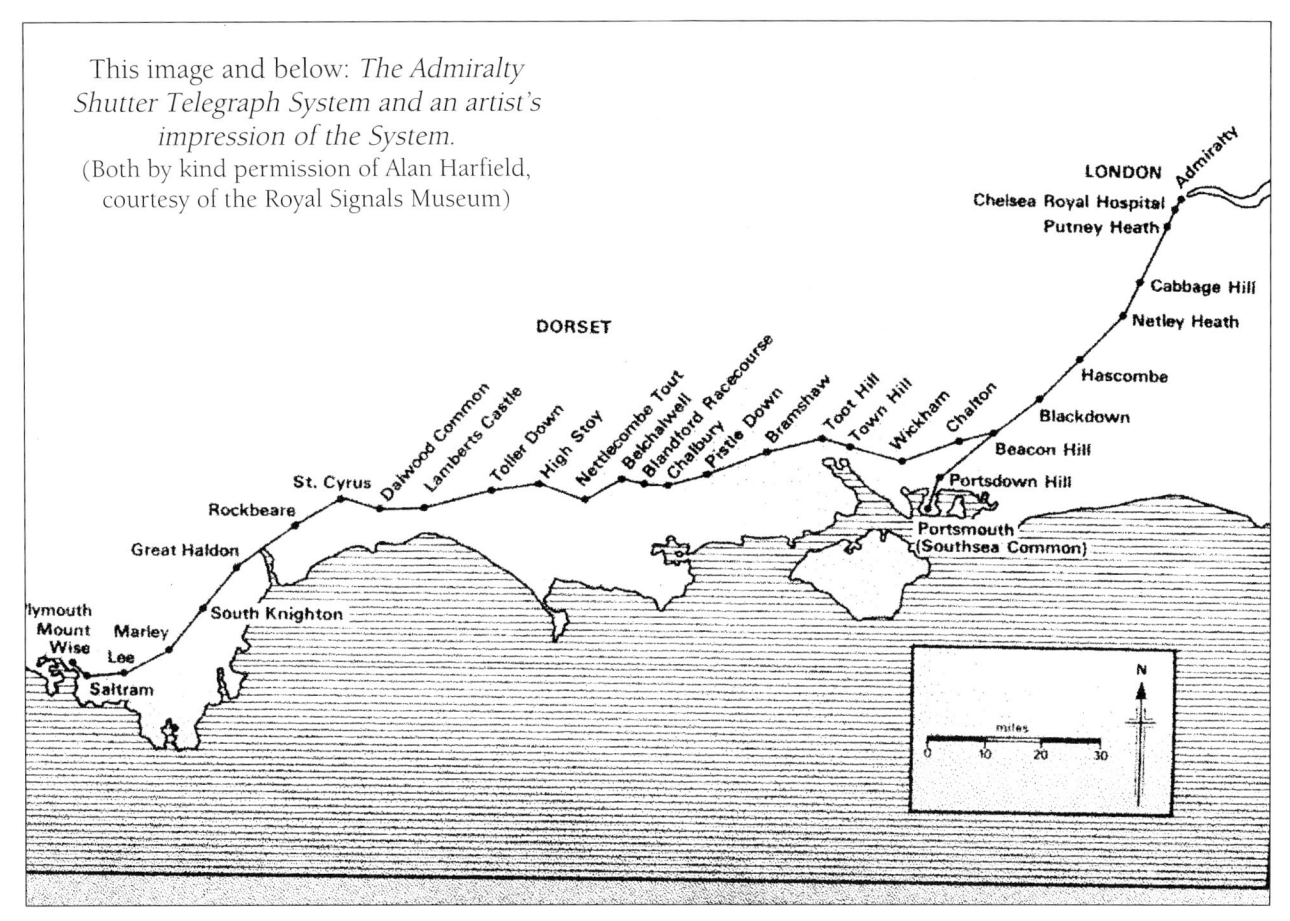

This image and below: The Admiralty Shutter Telegraph System and an artist's impression of the System. (Both by kind permission of Alan Harfield, courtesy of the Royal Signals Museum)

were lieutenants have risen to be generals and have gained the highest honours for valour and skill. The memories of those who have fallen will be enduringly preserved by the record of the Royal Naval Division and of the Royal Marines. They did not die in vain. I am proud to have been deputed by the King to welcome you back, after many perils and losses, to your native land, for which you have fought so well.

They were then dispersed to their respective Divisions and the Battalions ceased to exist. The final act of the Royal Naval Division took place on 7 June 1919 when a memorial, in the form of an obelisk containing two inscriptions was unveiled at the Blandford-Salisbury Road entrance to the camp. The dedication of the memorial reads:

IN MEMORY OF
THE COMMANDING OFFICER
OFFICERS AND MEN
OF THE COLLINGWOOD BATTN.
ROYAL NAVAL DIVISION
WHO FELL IN ACTION IN GALLIPOLI
ON 4TH JUNE 1915, WHEN THE
BATTN. WAS PRACTICALLY DESTROYED.

On the obverse side are the words:

THE COLLINGWOOD BATTALION COMPLETED
ITS TRAINING ON THESE DOWNS

From 1916 a German POW Camp was established on the eastern side of the camp and later a second POW Camp on the Milldown. POWs were hired out to local farmers and paid 4d. per hour. The Cook was paid 9d. per day!

In 1918 the RND was gradually converted to its new use by the Royal Flying Corps and ultimately to the newly formed Royal Air Force. At the time it was obviously intended as a permanent site as a light

Stud House.

Locations of American Hospitals in Blandford Camp 1944-45.

PIMPERNE AND THE MILITARY

railway was constructed from Blandford Station at a cost of £59 877, it was handed over to the Somerset and Dorset Line in 1919. The RAF camp increased its activities to include the Record Office RAF, Equipment and Personnel Depot and Discharge Centre. A 99-bed RAF Hospital was also established and later a Repatriation Camp to deal with the return of German POWs, the first RAF Band was formed here at this time. The personnel of the RAF Camp were particularly badly hit by the second influenza outbreak which began in September 1918 and lasted until December. There were 24 casualties, all buried in the military plot of the Town Cemetery.

At the end of 1919 the camp was closed, its wooden buildings were sold by auction and a number rebuilt as Village Halls, three of which were still in use in the 1990s - Tarrant Monkton, Tarrant Gunville and Tarrant Hinton. Apart from the adoption of names from the RND nothing tangible remains of the First World War Camp.

During the months of tension before the outbreak of the Second World War preparations were made for mobilisation and Blandford Camp was developed as a tented training camp. A photograph taken in August 1939 shows over 100 marquee tents and nearly 500 smaller ones and recruits had to cope not only with their new surroundings, but also with bad weather when the ground became a sea of mud. The wooden hutted camp was constructed in 1939/40 and was occupied first by Royal Artillery, becoming a transit camp after Dunkirk. It became a battle training camp, anti-aircraft units were trained there and it later held a prisoner of war camp.

It was in February 1943 that a lone German aircraft dropped several bombs, causing some damage to the camp cookhouse and the Camp Commandant, Brigadier H.S. Woodhouse, who was also Joint Managing Director of the local brewery, died during the air raid.

In April 1944 the camp again changed roles to become a hospital site with five American-run hospitals especially set up to deal with casualties from the June 1944 invasion of France and subsequent battles. 19 500 patients passed through these hospitals up to the end of the war, many brought back via Tarrant Rushton Airfield, as many as 500 casualties arriving in one night.

The Hospitals closed after VE day and the Roosevelt Park was opened on Memorial Day 30 May 1945, dedicated by Col Leonard D. Heaton US Army, 'To the everlasting memory of our fellow soldiers, at home or abroad, who gave their lives in this war, so that we who live may share in the future a free and better world... '.

After the Second World War Blandford Camp remained in military hands and trained national servicemen for the Royal Artillery, Royal Army Service Corps, Royal Electrical and Mechanical Engineers and the Army Catering Corps. In 1960 its permanent long-term link with the Royal Corps of Signals was established when 30th Signal Regiment moved into the camp. In 1967 the School of Signals moved from Catterick into tailor-made permanent buildings here and in 1995 the camp grew to accommodate all trainees of the Corps and the headquarters of the Signal-Officer-in-Chief. The Camp is today the focal point of military communications and the permanent home of the Corps.

During the period 1948 until the early 1960s Blandford Camp became well known as a site for motor cycle racing and became established as one of the best circuits in England. The popularity of the sport, the circuit and the scheduled events drew large crowds and it was estimated that an average crowd of 30 000 persons attended each meeting. In 1950 Geoff Duke arrived on the scene riding a Featherbed Norton and set a new lap record of 91 mph.

The racing at Blandford Camp continued until the early 1960s when it suffered some serious crashes including one in which a competitor in a 500cc Formula Three race finished up on the Guard House roof after which the camp circuit was closed.

In 1988 the Royal Corps of Signals launched a New Museum Project and fund-raising began. As a result of this project a purpose built extension was opened by the HRH The Princess Royal in 1992 and fund-raising continued until, with the aid of a National Lottery grant, the present Museum was ready and officially opened in May 1997.

Right and top: Cap badges of Drake and Howe Battalions.

155

Programme and T.T. Race, c. 1949.

SUBSCRIBERS

Grace Broomfield Abbey, Pimperne, Dorset
Stuart C. F. Adam
Roy Adam M.B.E., Pimperne born
Mr and Mrs R. D. Allan, Pimperne, Dorset
The Argles family, Pimperne, Dorset
Betty Attwool, Pimperne, Dorset
Mrs Anne Babington
Christine M. and Andrew J. Ballard, Pimperne, Dorset
Mrs Susan M. Banks,
Mr A. Bartlett, Pimperne, Dorset
Jack and Stephanie Beggs, Pimperne, Dorset
Mrs M. J. Best, Pimperne, Dorset
Roy Biles, Pimperne, Dorset
Peter and Valerie Boyt, Pimperne, Dorset
Diana F. Bozie, Blandford Forum, Dorset
Colin Brett, Winchburgh, West Lothian
Vera Brett, Pimperne, Dorset
Brian Brett, Llanelli, South Wales
Keith B. Churchill, Pimperne, Dorset
D. and J. Coles,
Mr Keiron Collier, Pimperne, Dorset
Christine Corry (née Morris), Pimperne, Dorset
Geoff and Christine Coull, Blandford, Dorset
Rachel Croft, Knaresborough, N. Yorkshire
Richard and Brian Cuff, Blandford, Dorset
Mary Cumming, Pimperne, Dorset
Mrs Jean Dalton, The Old Village Hall, Pimperne, Dorset
Rachel Daniel, Henley-on-Thames
Dee and Gordon Day, Pimperne, Dorset
Mrs Beryl Day, Pimperne, Dorset
Rex C. Dennis, Pimperne, Dorset
Alan G. Dennis, Pimperne, Dorset
J.G. and I. W. Dowdeswell, Pimperne, Dorset
Nancy C. J. Dowling, Blandford Forum, Dorset
Martin E. Draycott, Pimperne, Dorset
Michael Drayton, Odiham, Hants./formerly of Pimperne

Peter and Doris Duncan, Pimperne, Dorset
S. M. E. Dunford, Dover, Kent
J. K. and L. J. Dunn, Pimperne, Dorset
Chris Dyer, Pimperne, Dorset
Tony and Beryl Edmonds, Pimperne, Dorset
Crispin and Sara Ellis, Wimborne, Dorset
Rick and Barbara Ellis, Pimperne, Dorset
Hilary Ellis JP, Southwick, Sussex
Geoff and Jaqueline Exley, Pimperne, Dorset
Miss Tracey Finlay, Pimperne, Dorset
Mike and Liz Flanagan, Pimperne, Dorset
Darren Gale, Pimperne, Dorset
Colin and Sonia Gale, Pimperne 2000
Mike, Celia, Katherine and Anthony Gilbert, Blandford, Dorset
K. J. Goodfield, Pimperne, Dorset
Lynn Stella Gregory-Hudson,
Bernice and Dick Griffin, Pimperne, Dorset
Phyllis M. Gulbins, Pimperne, Dorset
Dick and Joan Hall, Blandford Forum, Dorset
Viveca and David Hart, Pimperne, Dorset
Sue and Ray Hatchard, Pimperne, Dorset
Peter J. Hawkins, Blandford St Mary, Dorset
Leonard R. Hawkins, Tarant Keynstone, Dorset
Stella Hayward, Verwood, Dorset
Mr J and Mrs P Hearne, Pimperne, Dorset
Edwin Hewitt, Pimperne, Dorset
Catherine Hewitt (née Brett), Hengoed, South Wales
Joan Holland, Pimperne, Dorset
Geoffrey Holland, London
Mr and Mrs D. Holman,
K. H. P. and K. I. Honner, Pimperne, Dorset
Ann Howland, Pimperne, Dorset
Mrs Ivy Hudson, Pimperne, Dorset
Mr Ronald V. M. Hughes, Pimperne, Dorset
Mary Hunt, Chudleigh, Devon
Martin G. Hunt, formerly of Pimperne, Dorset
Nicholas Hely Hutchinson, Pimperne, Dorset

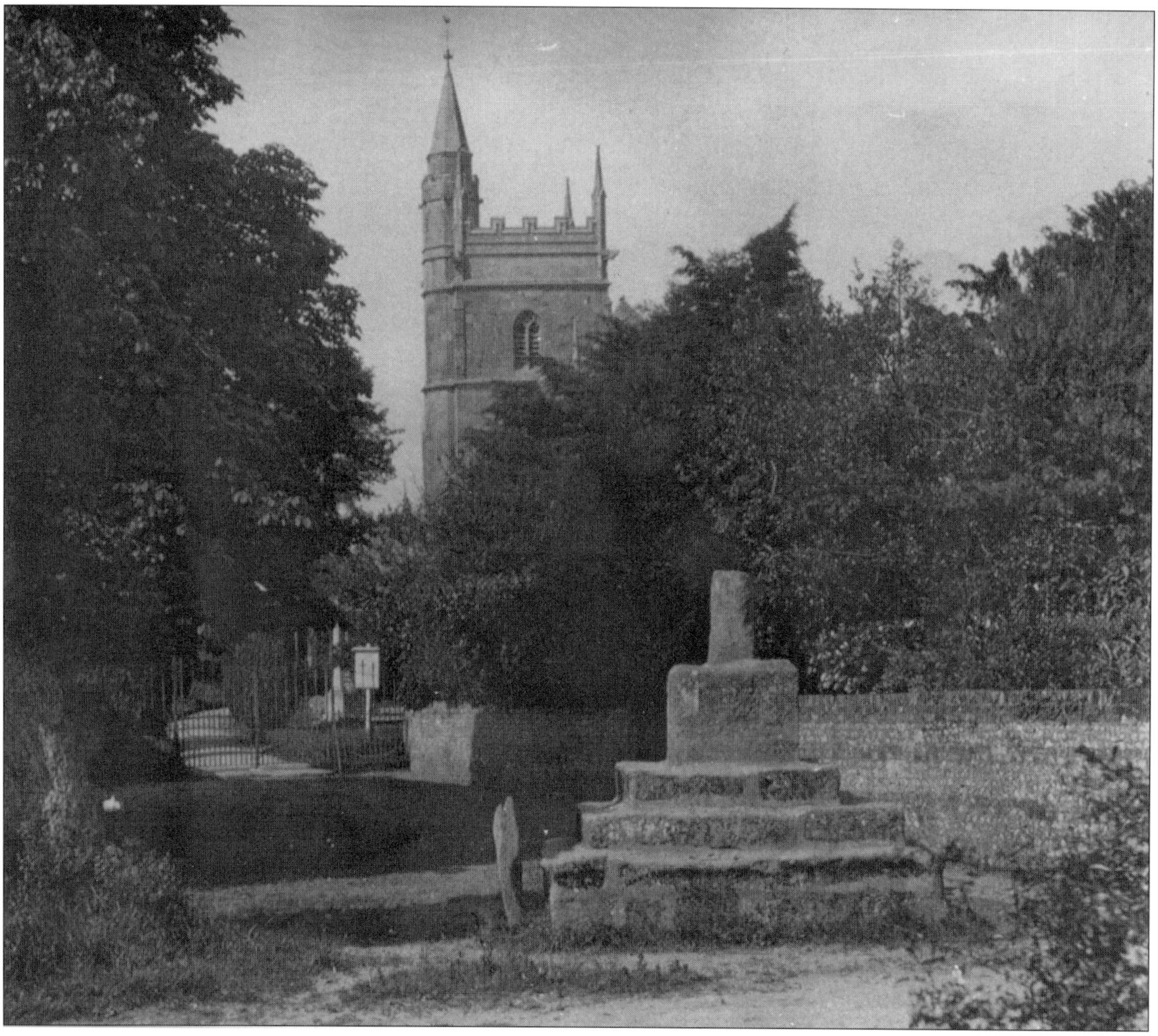

SUBSCRIBERS

John, Julia, Graham and Martin Jenner, Pimperne, Dorset
Thomas Owen Joyce, Blandford St Mary, Dorset
Reg, Thelma and Philip Joyce, Blandford Forum, Dorset
Jackie and John King, Pimperne, Dorset
Robert King, Pimperne, Dorset
Tine and Wigbert Koops, Den Helder, Netherlands
Pauline J. Langdown, Blandford, Dorset
Mrs Alice Langdown, Pimperne, Dorset
Graham C. Langdown, Cranborne, Dorset
Mr C. P. Langdown, Pimperne, Dorset
Myrtle Leak
Mr and Mrs P. Lester-Shaw, Letton Park, Pimperne, Dorset
Russell and Lucy Lucas-Rowe, Newfield Farm, Pimperne, Dorset
A. G. Lukins and Co., Pimperne, Dorset
Stan and Judy Martin, Pimperne, Dorset
Mrs Hilda Martin, Pimperne, Dorset
Ann Matthews, Pimperne, Dorset
Brian and Mary Matthews, Pimperne, Dorset
Frazer and Samantha McCarthy, Pimperne, Dorset
Mr G. P. Meadowcroft, Pimperne, Dorset
Vic and Sue Miles (née Bennett), Pimperne, Dorset
Mrs Ruth H. Miller (née Thorne), Grandad & Uncle were Blacksmiths of Pimperne
Suzannah F. Morris
Bill and Barbara Morris (née Legge), Sutton Coldfield/formerly of Pimperne
Gerald and Susan Mosney, Ex Pimperne, Dorset
L. Brian Moss, Pimperne, Dorset
Steve and Chris Mowlam, Weymouth, Dorset
Jim and Joan Mowlam, Weymouth, Dorset
Jean M. Newell, Pimperne, Dorset
Peter, Deborah, Kevin and Lisa Noyce, Pimperne, Dorset
Lieutenant Colonel Michael D. Oliver, Pimperne, Dorset
Frederick C. Osment, Pimperne, Dorset
Mrs Sylvia Packham, Pimperne, Dorset
David and Eunice Paculabo, Pimperne, Dorset
Mr Jonathan and Mrs Janet Parker, Pimperne, Dorset
Mrs H. Pollard, Sherborne, Dorset
Mr A. Cyril Randall, Poole, Dorset
Muriel and Malcolm Reed, Blandford, Dorset
Elizabeth Reed, Sutton, Surrey
Mrs Doreen Ridout, Stourpaine, Blandford, Dorset
Kathleen Riggs, Pimperne, Dorset
Phyllis Riley, Pimperne, Dorset
K. B. Roberts, Pimperne, Dorset
Helen Rogers, Pimperne, Dorset
Mrs Lynne Saunders, Pimperne, Dorset
A. and K. Scriven, Weymouth, Dorset
Sue Simmonds and Family,
Peter A. Slocombe, Pimperne, Dorset
Ron and Trudy Smith, Pimperne, Dorset
Beth Stephens, Fleet, Hants./formerly of Pimperne, Dorset
Mrs Jane M. Stockdale, Pimperne, Dorset
A. A. and J. A. Suggitt, Pimperne, Dorset
John and Joyce Tanner and Charlotte, The Old Bakery, Pimperne, Dorset
Mr G. J. and Mrs K. Y. Tapper, Priory Gardens, Pimperne, Dorset
Jane Taylor, Pimperne, Dorset
Claire Taylor, Pimperne, Dorset
Norah Taylor, Pimperne, Dorset
Michael Taylor, Pimperne, Dorset
Robert Taylor, Pimperne, Dorset
Rory Taylor, Pimperne, Dorset
Tracy Taylor, Pimperne, Dorset
William Taylor, Pimperne, Dorset
Thomas Taylor, Pimperne, Dorset
The Blake Family, Pimperne, Dorset
Cyril and Joyce Thornes, Pimperne, Dorset
Paul Tory, Charlton Marshall, Dorset
Shareen Trim (née Macey), Dorchester
Mr and Mrs J. C. Truswell, Blandford, Dorset
Helen Turner, Putney, London
M. and J. S. Vacher, Pimperne, Dorset
Hazel Vieten, St Leonard, Hants./formerly of Pimperne, Dorset
Leonard C. Vincent, Pimperne, Dorset
Mr M. Waite, Pimperne, Dorset
John F. W. Walling, Newton Abbot, Devon
Mrs Maureen Wareham, Blandford, Dorset
Alan and Margaret Warwick, Pimperne, Dorset
Fred Waterman, Pimperne, Dorset
Stephen Waterman, Deddington, Oxford
Graham and Lyn Wicks, Pimperne, Dorset
Mrs M. Wilks, Park View, Kenton, Exeter, Devon
John Willis-Fisher, Pimperne, Dorset

AVAILABLE TO BUY NOW IN THE SERIES

The Book of Addiscombe, In Celebration of a Croydon Parish • Various
The Book of Bampton, A Pictorial History of a Devon Parish • Caroline Seward
The Book of Bickington, From Moor to Shore • Stuart Hands
The Parish Book of Cerne Abbas, Abbey and After • Vivian and Patricia Vale
The Book of Chittlehampton, A North Devon Parish • Various
The Book of Cornwood and Lutton, Photographs and Reminiscences • Compiled by the People of the Parish
The Ellacombe Book, A Portrait of a Torquay Parish • Sydney R. Langmead
The Book of Grampound with Creed • Amy Bane and Mary Oliver
The Book of Hayling Island and Langstone • Various
The Book of High Bickington, A Devon Ridgeway Parish • Avril Stone
The Book of Helston, Ancient Borough and Market Town • Jenkin with Carter
The Book of Ilsington, A Photographic History of the Parish • Dick Wills
Lanner, A Cornish Mining Parish • Scharon Schwartz and Roger Parker
The Book of Lamerton, A Photographic History • Ann Cole and Friends
The Book of Loddiswell, Heart of the South Hams • Various
The Book of Manaton, Portrait of a Dartmoor Parish • Compiled by the People of the Parish
The Book of Meavy, Dartmoor Parish, Village and River • Pauline Hemery
The Book of Minehead with Alcombe • Hilary Binding and Douglas Stevens
The Book of North Newton, In Celebration of a Somerset Parish • Robins & Robins
The Book of Plymtree, The Parish and its People • Tony Eames
The Book of Porlock, A Pictorial Celebration • D. Corner
Postbridge – The Heart of Dartmoor • Reg Bellamy
The Book of Priddy, A Photographic Portrait of Mendip's Highest Village • Various
South Tawton and South Zeal with Sticklepath, 1000 Years Below the Beacon • Roy and Ursula Radford
The Book of Torbay, A Century of Celebration • Frank Pearce
Widecombe-in-the-Moor, A Pictorial History of a Dartmoor Parish • Stephen Woods
Uncle Tom Cobley and All, Widecombe-in-the-Moor • Stephen Woods
Woodbury, The Twentieth Century Revisited • Roger Stokes

SOME OF THE MANY TITLES AVAILABLE 2001

The Book of Bickleigh • Barrie Spencer
The Book of Blandford Forum • Various
The Book of Constantine • Various
The Book of Dawlish • Frank Pearce
The Book of Hemyock • Various
The Book of Hurn • Margaret Phipps
The Lustleigh Book • Tim Hall
The Book of Rattery • Various
The Book of Publow with Pensford • Various
The Book of Severn • Various
The Book of South Stoke • Various
The Book of Sparkwell • Pam James
The Book of Stourton Caundle • Philip Knott
The Book of Watchet • Compiled by David Banks
The Book of West Huntspill • Various

For details of any of the above titles or if you are interested in writing your own community history, please contact: Community Histories Editor, Halsgrove House, Lower Moor Way, Tiverton Business Park, Tiverton, Devon EX16 6SS, England. Tel: 01884 243242/e-mail:sales@halsgrove.com